ENDORSE

The Lonely Soldier by Tope Pearson

What can I say about 'The Lonely Soldier' by Tope Pearson..........a very action packed and fruitful read with all the threads and trains of thoughts rooted in the scriptures. We were constantly being asked to look back to the book of books: the glorious word of God, as any good driver should be encouraged to look in his rear view mirrors. The book challenges the big issues of today using great biblical illustrations. It also reminds us in this fast-changing world with all the uncertainties, that God is in complete control and nothing takes him by surprise. Sobering and thought provoking, challenging us to find our place in the body of the Messiah as a good soldier..........2 Timothy 2:3-4... You therefore must endure hardship as a good soldier of Jesus Christ. No-one engaged in warfare entangles himself with the affairs of this life, that he may please him who enlisted him as a soldier. Ecclesiastes 1:9. What has been will be again, what has been done will be done again; there is nothing new under the sun.

Reverend Arthur O'Malley,
Senior Pastor of Eastgate Church, Scotland

Events in our world are moving so quickly that it is getting more and more difficult to process them, even when we are alert. This book will help you to process all that is happening, and also prepare you for all that lies ahead.

The Bible is wonderfully prophetic, so Tope Pearson leads us to consider all the Global happenings in the light of the Scriptures. This reinforces what we know in our hearts, that the Lord is in control, knowing the end from the beginning.
Lonely Soldier needs to be read prayerfully and shared.

Reverend Brenda Taylor,
Founder of Dovetail Shalom Ministries, UK

Surviving as an 'awake' believer is not easy today, so this book is for people who feel isolated in their church and want to be better equipped for the battles ahead.

Melanie Symonds, Founding Editor,
HEART Publications, UK

The Lonely Soldier

Is your church awake or asleep in the end times?

Tope Pearson

Foreword by Brenda Taylor

ISBN: 978-1-7396070-2-9

Take note that the name anti-christ and related names are not capitalised. We choose not to acknowledge him, even to the point of violating grammatical rules.

Cover design by: Ronna Fu
Photography by: Stijn Swinnen and Aurelien Faux

❧ TABLE OF CONTENTS ❧

❦ ACKNOWLEDGMENTS ❧

I would first of all like to give a big thanks to our brother Mark Cunningham, who spent valuable time proofreading and editing this book. I am very grateful to Tim Pearson, my loving husband, for his heart knowledge on the End-Time subject matter and critiquing this book. Thanks also to Christian Walker, my dear son for some last-minute proofreading in certain parts. I would like to give a big thanks to our dear friend Jim Penberthy, for his encouraging feedback and final suggestions. A big thank you to both Bryan and Judith Spence, our spiritual mentors, for introducing us to the Galilean Wedding message and meaning. Thanks to Pastor Arthur O'Malley and Pastor Brenda Taylor, who both endorsed this book, and especially to Pastor Brenda for writing the Foreword. I thank those valuable parts of the Body of Christ who have been covering me in prayer in the process of writing. I also thank You Holy Spirit, for continuing to be both my helper and Senior Partner. All glory goes to King Jesus, to whom I say, *"come LORD, quickly come"* (Revelation 22).

✂ DEDICATION ✂

I dedicate this book to all who have felt a sense of loneliness along your journey through life or were adversely affected, when you were unable to get together with loved-ones during the first global lockdown in history. This book is also for those concerned about what is still to come in a world of uncertainty.

"...Do not weep! See, the Lion of the tribe of Judah, the Root of David, has triumphed" (Revelation 5:5).

✥ FOREWORD ✥

Loneliness can be personal, but also a 'people group' can be targeted to be cancelled, isolated, and therefore, in one sense, lonely.

This has been happening systematically with Christians across the globe. There is a persecution which can only get worse with the formation of the One World Church, led by the Pope. True Christians are a real threat to this organisation, because of our stand for Jesus Christ. The Bible has prophesied this will happen, and apostate groups will be part of it, and partner with the Anti-Christ. Loneliness and persecution are challenging, but great grace will be ours, and no-one said the end-time birth pangs would be easy.

We need to be strong, and of good courage: we need to be in fellowship with like-minded believers, and take a stand for the Kingdom! Christ will be with us, and loneliness will be a necessary part of 'being in the world, but not of it'.

Events in our world are moving so quickly that it is getting more and more difficult to process them, even when we are alert. This book will help you to process all that is happening, and also prepare you for all that lies ahead.

The Bible is wonderfully prophetic, so Tope Pearson leads us to consider all the Global happenings in the light of the Scriptures. This reinforces what we know in our hearts, that the Lord is in control, knowing the end from the beginning. Lonely Soldier needs to be read prayerfully and shared.

Reverend Brenda Taylor,
Founder of Dovetail Shalom Ministries, UK

❧ INTRODUCTION ❧

***Do you Feel Something is Missing in
Today's Church Teaching?
How Close are we to the End Time?***

TOPE PEARSON

Do you feel like a lonely soldier? Have you been involved in church life but feel there is something missing? Perhaps you feel there should be more preaching or teaching on the *End Times* and some guidance on how you could prepare, without panic and fear. Well, you are not alone. Although I can empathise with church leadership around the world, who may be apprehensive to teach on the *Last Days*, due to varied interpretations and not wanting to appear to be scare mongering or dividing the Body of Christ, I personally have discerned the need to search out scriptures, as well as weigh up teaching from various Christian pastors and leaders, who have dared to speak out.

I have written this book, started 2017, in order to walk with you on your journey of discovery on how close we really are to the *End Times,* providing useful tips on what you may do to get ready, in these crucial times we are living in. Is the standard church structure working anymore or should we be looking at the early church model in the book of Acts, with believers moving closer together in prayer and personal life challenges?

The Collins Dictionary defines loneliness as *'the unhappiness that is felt by someone because they do not have any friends or do not have anyone to talk to'.* Some people may however, have many friends but describe their state of mind as feeling lonely due to the fear of losing a loved-one or being left desolate. Loneliness from a spiritual perspective, could also be connected to what is known as the 'orphan heart'. This is a complex issue, which may go right back to birth or the lack of a loving father or mother. A person with an orphan heart, for example, may be told by another well-meaning person, *"I am not hugging people anymore; it is nothing personal, but I would like to keep my boundaries".* However, the person hearing those words, actually hear the lies of the enemy whisper, *"Jesus does not love me anymore, because I am not worthy."* Instantly, rejection and offence enter into the existing hole within their soul, because they may not be secure in Christ's love, which only God can fix. In such cases, inner healing is required.

Generally, when you are certain that you are heading in a direction where there is light at the end of the tunnel, you tend to feel less lonely on the journey. The world has entered unprecedented times, whereby the very first global lockdown occurred in 2020. Everyone in the entire population, unlike ever before, were forced to abide by a new set of governmental rules as to what they could and could not do and who they could and could not see. There was a mixture of experiences, some people reporting good things, like they used the opportunity to slow down their hectic lifestyle and some married couples became closer through the trials. Many people struggled during the COVID lockdown measures, most especially, the single people I spoke to, who were furloughed, confirmed they were bored, lost their peace and felt lonely and depressed. Sadly, the UK introduced a national Suicide Day in September 2021.

The LORD created us to have a relationship with Him, first and foremost, and then with each other. He blessed us with a free-will, to cultivate, to rule and procreate. In this season, all these things are being slowly eroded by laws and guidance thrust upon the people of the land. The whole world is still in a state of confusion and one could argue that the biggest, yet most subtle attack is happening to the human body, soul and spirit today, like never before. Although I understand things need to be done within reason, to mitigate the impact of a newly defined pandemic or disaster, many people believe there is something more sinister underlying here. After all, it is abnormal to stop being who you are meant to be and what you are meant to do. Sooner or later loneliness, boredom and frustration sets in and something has to give, especially in the area of mental health.

Loneliness in society is not just a recent problem and we will see from this book that it resonated since the fall of mankind. According to data from the Office for National Statistics (ONS, April 2018), throughout 2016/17, 5% of adults in England reported feeling lonely "often" or "always". Younger adults aged 16-24 reported feeling lonely more often than older age groups. People in poor health or with conditions described as "limiting" were also often at high risk of feeling lonely. A previous study by Age UK (2014) had found that two-fifths of all older people, accounting for roughly 3.9 million people, have the television as their main company. Of wider concern is that these figures are much higher for people with disabilities. According to Scope two-thirds (67%) of disabled people have felt lonely in the past year, rising to three-quarters (76%) for working age disabled people (December, 2017).

In response to the growing challenge of loneliness, the UK government had undertaken a concerted effort to raise awareness of loneliness and isolation, dismantle stigma, and offer practicable guidance on delivering integrated services and care. In January 2018 the Prime Minister (PM) announced the long-awaiting Government plan to tackle loneliness. The PM appointed a ministerial lead on loneliness and the allocation of a dedicated fund.

However, despite these steps, it is clear that further progress is needed on tackling the structural determinants and the devastating impact of loneliness. According to the Royal College of General Practitioners (RCGP), the 1.1 million Britons who are estimated to be experiencing chronic loneliness are 50% more likely to die prematurely than people with active social relationships. In 2021, there were 6,538 registered suicides in the UK (ONS, December 2022). Research also shows that every £1 invested in tackling loneliness can save £3 in health costs [Source: Campaign to End Loneliness].

I quote Rabbi Jason Sobel in Kathie Lee Gifford's book called *The Rock, the Road and the Rabbi*, as he makes reference to the woman with the issue of blood in Mark 5:25-34, who due to her condition was made an outcast in Israel. – *"The root of all sin goes back to the garden of Eden. The result of Adam and Eve's disobedience was exile for them and all their descendants after them. Living in exile means living in a perpetual state of disconnection and separation that ultimately leads to death if not remedied. There are four aspects to exile: spiritual, emotional, relational and physical."*

If there was to be strife in any relationship whether between us and God or when two close people separate or disagree on values, it is not only painful but can leave an empty void. One could argue, there seems to be 'two' different types of detached people in the world. The world appears more divided and there is an impression of a divisive spirit at work, separating families, friends, colleagues and neighbours on matters concerning this world today. BREXIT, LGBTQ and transgender, Black Lives Matter, The British Monarchy, USA Democrats and Republicans, Islamic Extremists, COVID19 injection and anti-vaxxers, Israel and Palestinians, Russia and Ukraine, China and Taiwan, abortion, euthanasia, religion, cost of living crisis and climate issues. These 'divide and rule' tactics were used by Hitler in the days of the Nazis and you should wonder if a similar tactic is being used by the unseen powers today.

Look around you and open your eyes. There is talk of a 'One World' government, economy and religion emerging. Will this particular 'one world order' prevent countries or individuals who do not conform to its regime, from trading or doing what they feel is best for the people of the land? During the times when Leprosy was common, God's people would have still gathered together to worship Him and told the Lepers to stay away (Leviticus chapters 12 to 13). However, we are in a period where churches can now be told to stop meeting or meet with severe restrictions, which quenches the Holy Spirit. Are we in the last days Daniel prophesied in Daniel chapters 2 and 7? Could we be fast approaching the beginning of the seven-year Tribulation, known as 'Jacob's Trouble', which is designed for the salvation of unbelieving Israel? Whatever stage of the End Time prophetic calendar we are, I truly believe we may be at the latter stages of the pregnant woman's labour contraction pains scenario, which our LORD Jesus warned us about in Matthew 24:8. I strongly sense both the anti-christ and false prophet are alive today and they want the true Church (Ekklesia) removed, so they can further deceive the nations into the abomination which provokes the wrath of God. Although I admit to sway on the pre-Tribulation (pre-Millennium) argument, that is, Jesus will take His Bride (the Church) with Him before the seven-year Tribulation, regardless of whether you and I are still here on earth when it happens, there will be a supernatural acceleration to the *Great Tribulation*.

There are questions you should be asking yourself right now, including whether the division and strife in the world is making you feel lonely or are you soldiering through, with the right support?

> *No one serving as a soldier gets entangled in civilian affairs, but rather tries to please his commanding officer.*   2 Timothy 2:4

The Apostle Paul was not suggesting you drop your secular work, because even he still did some tent making work, whilst serving Jesus, so as not to depend on anyone else for his sustenance. Nevertheless, he listened and obeyed Jesus' teaching and prepared himself as a soldier would, for the *End Times*, even two thousand years ago. Paul knew those who chose to live a Godly life would suffer persecution and did not shy away from talking about it to the churches in his province. When my husband, Tim, was a soldier in the British army, he benefitted from receiving clear instructions from his commanding officer, and felt valued, connected and had a focus. Who are you following, man or our LORD Jesus, who is our ultimate Commanding Officer? As soldiers of Christ, we are in His mighty army together and ought not to be lonely, knowing we wear the full armour of God and our fellow officers (brothers and sisters in Christ) have our back, Ephesians 6:10-18.

The most important question should be, *"am I saved?"* This is a valid point because when Jesus returns, the issue will not be whether you are for or against the complex issues we face, but if you are among the saved or unsaved? If you are saved, then you are a soldier, fighting in the midst of isolation, like the person of Lot, in the Bible. I am not referring to the type of soldier who dresses in army uniform and carries physical deadly weapons, as a form of defense and attack during times of war. I mean the type of solider mentality, who knows who he or she is in Christ, understands the sign of the times and that he or she is among the remnant. The weapons of warfare you fight with are not carnal, but spiritual and powerful for pulling down strongholds through prayer, 2 Corinthians 10:4-6. Although, there will be times when you feel lonely and grieved along the journey, because the main battle is in the mind, you decide to stand firm in your faith and make your thoughts subject to Christ, as you understand that God's grace is sufficient for you, 2 Corinthians 12:9.

God has put a time-line on earth as we know it and used Sodom and Gomorrah as a lesson for us all. Approximately six hundred years before Jesus Christ was born, the Prophet Daniel interpreted the dream of King Nebuchadnezzar, and he talked about a large statue, from head to toe, making reference to the different powerful national governments which will establish themselves before Christ returns to rule the whole world forever. In these verses below, Daniel interprets what will happen in the times of the statue's toes. You see this in the world today:

Just as you saw that the feet and toes were partly of baked clay and partly of iron, so this will be a divided kingdom; yet it will have some of the strength of iron in it, even as you saw iron mixed with clay. As the toes were partly iron and partly clay, so this kingdom will be partly strong and partly brittle. And just as you saw the iron mixed with baked clay, so the people will be a mixture and will not remain united, any more than iron mixes with clay. Daniel 2:41-43

Daniel then goes on to say:

In the time of those kings, the God of heaven will set up a kingdom that will never be destroyed, nor will it be left to another people. It will crush all those kingdoms and bring them to an end, but it will itself endure forever. This is the meaning of the vision of the rock cut out of a mountain, but not by human hands—a rock that broke the iron, the bronze, the clay, the silver and the gold to pieces.

The great God has shown the king what will take place in the future. The dream is true and its interpretation is trustworthy.   Daniel 2:44-45

If then, we are currently living in the toes of that statue in the Book of Daniel, are you ready for the LORD's soon return?

In all of the world's perpetual sin and chaos, can you confidently say, 'I am the LORD's disciple and it is well with my soul?' If you can, the chances are you are doing well as Christ's soldier. If you are unable to say those words, then it is not too late. Read on, meditate on the scriptures I have included, and be encouraged. I may have written some things which may be considered controversial by some, but I am standing on God's word, as judgement must begin in the House of the LORD (1 Peter 4:17). Somehow, with all that the world is going through, I believe the LORD not only works for the good of those who love Him and whom He has called according to His purpose, He is also doing a new thing among us and wants us to perceive it, like Lot, so we do not feel we are on our own. God is with you, He is shaking the nations and has provided a way out for you, Romans 8:28, Isaiah 43:18-19 and Haggai 2:7. Jesus said:

"I have told you these things, so that in me you may have peace. In this world you will have trouble. But take heart! I have overcome the world." John 16:33

CHAPTER 1

❧ VEILED BY DECEPTION ❧

Lot looked around and saw that the whole plain of the Jordan toward Zoar was well watered, like the garden of the LORD, like the land of Egypt. (This was before the LORD destroyed Sodom and Gomorrah). So Lot chose for himself the whole plain of the Jordan and set out toward the east. The two men parted company: Abram lived in the land of Canaan, while Lot lived among the cities of the plain and pitched his tents near Sodom. Now the people of Sodom were wicked and were sinning greatly against the LORD.

GENESIS 13:10-13

There is a 'Lot' in all of us, including, those who strive to be righteous. The Hebraic meaning of the name Lot, is 'veiled' or 'hidden'. We all have the potential to be deceived. From the very beginning of age, when God made us, He has always loved us. Adam and Eve were deceived, by Satan, God's enemy, into eating the forbidden fruit in the Garden of Eden. This trickery led to man's first sin against God and is what brought about the fall of man. Sodom & Gomorrah as land, was obviously very attractive to the eye back then. Although there is nothing wrong with liking nice things, often we can make wrong decisions through lust and deception and become very lonely in the process. The question is, was Lot's face covered by hidden truth? Interestingly, wearing a mask over your face has become the 'new norm' today and has made people appear cold towards others. There is a feeling that people do not care about one another, or you cannot tell how another is feeling, so you do not bother to investigate. On a practical note, scientists have confirmed masks do not provide 100% protection and can actually deplete your ability to properly breathe in the God-given natural air. Also, many bacterial spores get caught within the mask, which is bad for your health. On a spiritual level, a mask conceals your true beauty and covers up your emotional expressions, including smiles, that God intended to light up the world. If people are unable to see someone else is hurting, how can they reach out a helping hand in that moment? On the flip side, God's enemy (the devil) does not want you to shine the glory of the Creator with your smile and laughter, instead he wants you to be miserable and be expressionless. The enemy likes to hide and hates our freedom. God has given you unique features, so others can recognise you. Wearing a mask covers your identity and brings confusion in society. Do you put on a *mask* at work, around your friends and other places? Are you making decisions based on half-truths or false information? This could be a symbol of the era of deception we are currently living in.

We are living in a world where lies are being spread

and believed through social media and dangerous propaganda by the official news media. You may see with your eyes, hear with your ears and even touch, to make sure something you are told is real, but it is really your preconceived understanding which causes you to believe a lie. Some advertisements are designed to entice our taste buds, which tempts us to become greedy and proud. A quick-fix, want, want, want now mentality is in our culture, never mind about the poor or less privileged, but let us live for me and 'keep up with the Jones'. Some people are now only communicating with others online or virtually and if not careful, could lose the ability to relate and become desensitised to how we respond to events in a way that makes us human. Also, some of the global elites are offering the world futuristic plans which seem attractive but deliberately go directly against God's teaching and laws.

Sodom and Gomorrah may have appeared lovely on the outside but what was going on the inside? We are told exactly what was going on behind the scenes by Prophet Ezekiel.

> Now this was the sin of your sister Sodom: She
> and her daughters were arrogant, overfed and
> unconcerned; they did not help the poor and needy.
> They were haughty and did detestable things before
> me. Therefore I did away with them as you have
> seen...   Ezekiel 16:49-50

There are just under eight billion people on this earth

and Jesus warned we will always have the poor among us, Matthew 26:11. James defined true religion to mean caring for widows and orphans and keeping oneself blameless from the world, James 1:27. Throughout the Bible, including Isaiah 58, God's heart shouts loudest for the poor and underdog in society. Yet it has been mentioned that some people who have reached the so-called top, are planning to curb the number of the global population, so there is less burden on society. Are you turning a blind-eye towards the destitute? Did you hear about the professional photojournalist named Kevin Carter, who won a prize for taking the photo known as 'The Struggling Girl', which had a hungry vulture staring at a skinny starving Sudanese girl, who was crouched over, probably crying for help? Later, Kevin Carter committed suicide in 1994. The newspapers suggest the reason behind him taking his life was because of the horrors he witnessed during his short career. [Source: The Guardian, Wed, 30 July 2014 by Eamonn McCabe].

What are you doing today that is detestable before God? Also, during the time of the Holocaust, as some of the Jewish people were being taken by train to the gas chambers, we hear that the local church increased their voices as they sang hymns, to drown out the screams of the victims about to be murdered. If you are a Christian believer, you are in the world but not of this world (John 17:16). We are merely passing through this earth. The current world is not the one we will live throughout eternity with God. Today we hear of some elite paying scientists to invent ways man can live longer, even if that means living on a different planet. We are heading for a 'bionic man' society through Artificial Intelligence (AI) to make super-humans who will indulge in more riches and power. Electric cars are planned to become super cars, where no human driver is required. This current earth is decaying but it is Jesus who has made all things new, and not man. Man may offer new technology as the answer, but even computers fail.

A quote by Elbert Hubbard:

"One machine can do the work of fifty ordinary men. No machine can do the work of one extraordinary man".

How many times have you looked over the garden fence and, in your heart, felt the grass is much greener on the other side?

Do not let your heart envy sinners, but always be zealous for the fear of the LORD.

There is surely a future hope for you, and your hope will not be cut off.   Proverbs 23:17-18

We live in a culture which is on a constant conveyor belt, looking for get-rich-quick schemes, the latest gadgets and partners, music artist or film stars to idolise, fantasise or gossip about. The concern is even many Christian believers have become descensitised to the sin in the world, that sadly, they fail to realise that they have already returned to 'Egypt'. Living in sin is a very lonely place. The Psalmist who wrote Psalm 139, knew what it was like to walk with God, then try to hide from Him when living sinfully. The poet had a deep journey experience with God, coming to understand that he had once believed the lie that he could choose not to be seen by his Creator, God Almighty. He then reveals how much more God knows man than he understands himself. He ends the song as though he does not trust his own heart and asks God to constantly test him, show him any deceit or crookedness within him, and lead him to a better way, which can only be God's way – the God who sees. The ultimate risk with being caught in a sinful mess, is the trickery it brings, so that you are not prepared for the soon return of our LORD.

I had a vision some years ago of people walking through an invisible church building, without a care in the world as they went about their daily lives. This was a description of people's indifference towards the things of God. The sad thing is, many people today are like the man named Uzzah, who touched the Ark of Covenant and died, 2 Samuel 6:7. Very few truly revere God, including those who attend church. When Jesus spoke to the seven churches in the Book of Revelation, He was very much referring to the End-Time church age, which includes the church you attend today. Which of these seven churches in Revelation chapters one to three, would you best describe your church? Does your church appear to have a good reputation, populated mainly with unbelieving people playing church? Are you among the faithful few who can see what is happening, evaluating the situation, confronting sin and making a difference? Is the LORD commanding your church to wake up, and strengthen the things that remain, which were about to die, like He did with the church at Sardis in Revelation 3:2-3?

Using the Ten Commandments in Exodus 20:1-17, here are some examples of how the hearts of many, even Christian believers, have become veiled and how many are in danger of losing their soul.

> *"I am the LORD your God … You shall have no other gods before me…"*

The spirit of Baal is operating throughout the nations, hence why we need a spokesperson with the spirit of Elijah, to be a voice for God's people today and counter-attack. There are many false gods; those which are carved by human hands and other things, which may not be so obvious. A recent shocking example, which would have provoked God's anger, at the Commonwealth Games 2022 in Birmingham, UK, the ceremony opened with the unashamed worship of Baal, in the shape of a carved-out bull statue. This was a modern-day copy of the Israelites who rebelled against God, when they waited for Moses to come down from Mount Saini.

Money was meant for keeping us alive but many people worship money, including digital currency, as if it were a god. Children and pets can be idolised, if we are not careful. Also, the way you perceive things like your job, ministry, health and the medical profession - to name a few, could border on idolatry. God is a jealous God, therefore, nothing or no-one in our lives should be placed before or higher than God. Sadly, the punishment for breaking this first and greatest command has been meted out to successive generations. However, blessings come to those generations who love God with their whole being.

"You shall not misuse the name of the LORD..."

Many people today use the name Jesus or God, as a joke, swear or curse word in their everyday sentences. When you go to watch a movie, in many cases, the actors and actresses are blaspheming and you tend to laugh along with it. The question you need to ask yourself is, would you have such a person in your home in front of your children, or your church on Sunday morning saying the same things before the congregation? Is the LORD truly reverenced as holy in your heart?

"Remember the Sabbath day by keeping it holy..."

Whether you observe the Sabbath on a Saturday or a Sunday, remember Jesus Christ is the LORD of the Sabbath. Whatever the day of the week, it is a command to honour the seventh day as the LORD's day and rest each week. There was a time in the United Kingdom when you would have felt ashamed to not attend church or to go to work on a Sunday. Nowadays, anything goes, as stores, markets, pubs, leisure centres, extra-curriculum classes are all operating as normal and, in some cases, busier than the weekdays. The new generation do not know any different because they were born into this new culture, so do not ask any questions. More and more people are suffering from depression, anxiety, burn-out, strokes, heart attacks and some sadly dying due to working long hours and seven-day weeks. Remember, our God Himself, rested on the seventh day of creation. Are you better than Him? I think not.

Since the COVID19 pandemic, we can see how God is shaking not just the UK but all the nations. Everyone was forced to take some rest from activities, events and general business which may have kept them from honouring and worshipping the One and only God of the Universe. Even some ministries had become gods to Christian leaders who have had no choice but to lay it all down before the King of kings and take a sabbatical. Rest allows you to stop, reflect and depend on the Almighty God rather than your own strength and abilities. God created you first and foremost to have a relationship with Him. Are you resting in the finished work of the Cross?

> *"Honour your father and mother, so that you may live long in the land..."*

Lot was a type of adopted son to Abraham, following the loss of his parents at an early age. However, he did not honour Abraham when it came to choosing land.

31

Lot instead chose what looked better and perhaps more acres. Could this have been a test of honoring your father? This command is the only one which promises a reward – '...so that all may go well with you', Ephesians 6:2-3. Unfortunately, all did not go well for Lot after this, however, God not only protected Abraham and his household, He blessed them richly.

Government laws are restricting school teachers and parents in how they should discipline their own children, consequently, dishonour within families has become prevalent in the UK. It is no wonder some parents have decided to home-school their children, despite the challenges this brings.

In the words of Voddie T Baucham Jr, Author of Family Driven Faith: Doing what it takes to Raise Sons and Daughters who Walk with God, "We cannot continue to send our children to Caesar for their education and be surprised when they come home as Romans".

Unfortunately, many schools and other educational institutes teach children about sex and other inappropriate things which deprives them of their innocence at a very early age. Children are given the power to change their gender without their parent's consent. Men are now allowed in ladies public changing rooms if they identify themselves as a female in that moment. A lady in a female prison has been raped by a man who wanted to be identified as a woman. And still, social justice is being taught in schools in a twisted way to the point of living in a 'woke' society, in which the 19th Century three 'R's (reading, writing and arithmetic) are no longer a priority in school education. Some people are wondering why the teachers are not taking industrial action against these distorted things as oppose to or in addition to demanding an increase in wages.

Sexting is no longer just from a personal text message photo to another but is now on social media platforms where mums and dads may or may not see what their children are up to. How is this honouring your father and mother? If you are unable to respect your parents, how can you begin to esteem God?

"You shall not murder"

Many people knowingly or ignorantly are bringing their children up on games and videos where, if killing and murder were not the main part, it would be deemed boring or tame.

In the light of George Floyd's death in 2020, although I must admit, I still cannot bring myself to watch the nine minutes of the shameful barbaric cruelty in broad daylight towards a civilian, by a police officer, whose US taxes pay to protect people like George, I have not felt so disturbed and saddened by the way society has become in these last days. Despite some video games and films being much more violent than this incident, the way the whole world reacted to the Floyd murder, showed we were all dismayed and had time to reflect on what man has become. However, with increased hatred for one another, which causes the wars we see today across different nations, I believe too many people have become less sensitive to what our God-given human instinct tells us is clearly wrong or evil. Jesus taught us to love and forgive, even our enemies, although this is hard, the world would be a much better place if we all followed Christ and obeyed His teachings.

And for your lifeblood I will surely demand an accounting. I will demand an accounting from every animal. And from each human being, too, I will demand an accounting for the life of another human being.

Whoever sheds human blood, by humans shall their blood be shed; for in the image of God has God made mankind. Genesis 9:5-6

"You shall not commit adultery"

Marriage is God's institution, hence why the adversary continues to hate it and wants to destroy it. Many today are fornicating in so many different ways and looking for God's blessing in their sins. Some deliberately attend churches where the ministers do not challenge their blatant sinful life but rather commend it. See Romans chapter 1.

For the time will come when people will not put up with sound doctrine. Instead, to suit their own

desires, they will gather around them a great number
of teachers to say what their itching ears want to
hear.   2 Timothy 4:3

Adultery is a sin against God as well as against the marriage partner (Genesis 39:9). It is a form of sexual immorality. The more perverse types today involve men in prominent positions within society paying for prostitutes, orgies and sex slaves, including paedophilia, where many of the children have come through child trafficking. Adultery is not only having physical or oral sex with another person who is not your spouse, it is to look lustfully at other people or to desire a close relationship with them in order to fill in any missing gaps in your heart (Matthew 5:27-30). This also includes fantasising about another person. One needs wisdom in this delicate area because even if you did not set out to have an affair, merely being irresponsible about how much time you spend with the opposite sex could be perceived as having an 'emotional affair', which consequently hurts the other partner in the marriage. Do not give even an hint of sin (Ephesians 5:3).

The entertainment industry today is booming because even Christian believers sow into this field, giving in to watching singers half-dressed or dancing provocatively and celebrities undressing or having sex. A lot of church-goers today have become numb to the filth on our TV screens and on their smartphones, as they are bombarded with indecent adverts or suggestions to watch videos which are inappropriate for God's Holy people. The question is why is it alright to watch this during the week but Sunday morning in a church building, the same people would be the first to condemn such behavior if one of our natural or God-family members performed indecently on the stage? One of the main reasons Herod's illegitimate wife, Herodias, hated John the Baptist is because he dared to challenge rightfully their adulterous and sinful life (Mark 6:17-20). When you read about Jesus saying, *"You hypocrites!"* (Matthew 25:15), have you ever put yourself at the receiving end of those words? Or have you thought it was just for the Jewish people or the Pharisees of that day? Remember, your body is a temple of the Holy Spirit (1 Corinthians 6:19), so be a radical disciple and flee sexual immorality, like Joseph in Genesis 39:6-12.

"You shall not steal"

What are some of the modern ways of stealing? Human trafficking, which is a form of slavery is one way, which is happening today as we speak in more subtle ways, where people, including children are being sold on the 'black market'. Many we hear are dying either during transportation or in their positions they were being misused for, under oppressive slave masters. Identification (ID) theft is a growing problem today. Cyber-crime is on the increase, phishing and internet scams have never been so high. '419 Fraud' is also expanding, whereby the fraudster poses to be a genuine customer. An example of this could be a landlord trying to rent out a property and someone poses to be a potential tenant. The fraudster then tries to get the landlord to send money to a third party to transport the tenant's items over in advance, stating this money transfer would be better done by the landlord and only when this takes place, will they pay their deposit and rent in advance. If the landlord falls prey, he or she could lose hundreds or thousands. The fraudsters are making millions by stealing money in this sly and wicked way.

Subtle theft is becoming more common, targeting the vulnerable. Some leaseholders with humble savings today are being ripped off by freeholders who are presenting them with extortionate high bills; in the region of £100,000s for repairs and maintenance of the building. You would not even expect a corporate organisation to be wacked with such hefty bills but individuals, including those coming from a social housing past are being forced into debt-traps like these. The Bible warns against uneven scales, Proverbs 11:1.

"You shall not give false testimony against your neighbour"

Exaggeration and half-truths are a form of lying. Deception has crept in when you genuinely feel your lie was innocent and you find yourself having to lie again to cover up the lies before, which tend to lead to other sins. As already mentioned, there is so much fake news today, no-one knows what and who to believe. Technology is so advanced that people are manipulating photos and videos to promote propaganda and lies, which ultimately hurts individuals and their families. Royalty, Presidents and Prime Ministers are not even immune from being at the receiving end of this. Deception is no respecter of persons.

"You shall not covet..."

Coveting is to desire possession of someone else's belongings or relationship (Matthew 15:19). To break God's commandment inwardly is equivalent to breaking them outwardly (Matthew 5:21-30). Unfortunately, this is the commandment that when you break it, most of the other branches of sin arise, such as acting enviously by going after other people's items or relations with malicious intent and at the expense of the person who legitimately own those things or people. For example, to want someone else's car, job, house, new phone, partner, child or au pair, is wrong in God's eyes. Look at King David's covetous behaviour towards Bathsheba (Uriah's wife) in 2 Samuel 11:1-4 and see his prayer in Psalm 51.

These coveting desires also include all types of sexual immorality or fornication, which is sex outside of marriage. Remember, that somebody is someone else's daughter, son, sister, brother, mother, father, future wife or husband.

The commandments, *"You shall not commit adultery," "You shall not murder," "You shall not steal," "You shall not covet," and whatever other command there may be, are summed up in this one command: "Love your neighbor as yourself." Love does no harm to a neighbor. Therefore love is the fulfilment of the law.*

And do this, understanding the present time: The hour has already come for you to wake up from your slumber, because our salvation is nearer now than when we first believed.   Romans 13:9-11

God did not give His laws because He does not want us to enjoy ourselves, on the contrary, He made them to protect us because He loves us. God's word in the Holy Bible is a love story to mankind. From Genesis to Revelation, He is trying to communicate His undying love to you. Since we live in a fallen world, He has to test us, to see which of us truly love Him back. Relationship is a two-way thing, hence, the more you read the Bible, the more you get to know yourself, God and where things are heading in this world and the new one to come. Each trial for each person is different because God knows what you personally can handle. Deuteronomy 8 and James 1:2-4 explains this. In Exodus chapter 20, you will notice the first four commands are to do with our direct relationship with God and the other six are to do with our human relationships with others. Without God's law, there would be too much pain and anarchy, hence why most governments and high courts today base their laws and sentencing on God's Holy Bible.

For rebellion is like the sin of divination, and arrogance like the evil of idolatry.

Because you have rejected the word of the LORD, he has rejected you as king.   1 Samuel 15:23

Rebellion against God's laws is a form of witchcraft, so it pays to take time to ask Him for conviction of any sins you need to confess and repent.

Moses said to the people, "Do not be afraid. God has come to test you, so that the fear of God will be with you to keep you from sinning."   Exodus 20:20

During Queen Elizabeth II's reign on earth, she fought to uphold the Christian faith, which many nations have benefited from. Now she has gone to be with the LORD, we should expect compromise but at the same time, not give up in praying for those in authority. Which sins are you tolerating? Today, many people are calling right wrong and wrong right. To be a true Christian is really to be a true disciple of Christ. The question is, are you a convert or a disciple? Jesus commanded us to make disciples of all nations, Matthew 28:18. Converts tend to compromise and try fit in with the world's narrative, whilst fleeing persecution. However, disciples of Christ grow during suffering and stand up for what is right in God's eyes.

To the Jews who had believed him, Jesus said, "If you hold to my teaching, you are really my disciples. Then you will know the truth, and the truth will set you free." John 8:31-32

My first time of walking to the front of the stage, in

response to an alter-call was at a Billy Graham event in 1986, UK. I was still a teenager and had no idea why I was crying, I simply sensed an open heaven and the presence of God. When I returned back to my seat, some members of that Anglican church asked me why I went to the front and I shrugged my shoulders because I honestly did not have an answer. Then I went back into the 'world', whilst still attending church religiously. It was not until fifteen years later, several women of God sacrificed their time to disciple me; strengthening me through God's word on a regular basis. Every new soldier in battle requires training and coaching, in readiness to be exposed to the enemy's ferocious attacks.

The church today must learn from the church at Pergamum, in Revelation 2:12-17 and see it as a severe warning. Like now, the church lived in a hostile environment, where satanic practices were common place. Despite strong persecution, which led to the death of one of their faithful church members, the majority of the congregation remained in the faith. However, there were some who followed false teaching and tolerated sinful acts by other members of the church. The Bible makes it clear how sin in the church must be confronted. See Matthew 18:15-18. However, most of today's churches have come away from practicing church discipline and shy away from discipleship because in doing so, they may not appear politically correct. I acknowledge there are some sins committed as a result of mental illness, and we must treat those issues with sensitivity and love.

However, it must be made clear that sin is sin, in sincere brokenness and not a boastful spirit, which celebrates it. Also, we must not allow the world to teach the church what we can and cannot say from God's word openly in the church, so as not to offend. How do we know that as a result of speaking the truth in love, we may be giving an opportunity for sinners to truly repent and be saved? Afterall, God's word is both living and active; sharper than a double-edged sword, Hebrews 4:12-13. As a consequence of tolerating the rebellious groups and refusing to exercise church discipline, the church of Pergamum shared in the guilt and experienced the LORD's judgement. Jesus, then gave them a chance to repent, so He can redeem them. Likewise, the same LORD is giving the churches today, a chance to turn away from the sin of compromise, so we do not have to go through the Tribulation along with unrepentant Israel.

> See to it, brothers and sisters, that none of you has
> a sinful, unbelieving heart that turns away from
> the living God. But encourage one another daily, as
> long as it is called "Today," so that none of you may
> be hardened by sin's deceitfulness. We have come
> to share in Christ, if indeed we hold our original
> conviction firmly to the very end. Hebrews 3:12-14

Hold onto Jesus' word and put them into practice today. To be radical for Christ means first opening your natural and spiritual eyes, discerning what the enemy is trying to lure your soul into and immediately stepping away from or shutting down whatever may cause you or others around you to stumble. See Genesis 39. Take some time to ask the LORD to help you to unveil your heart today. Reflect on each of God's commands, and repent by making practical changes to protect you and your loved-ones. A good starting place could be for you to change the TV channels you watch to a Christian-based box. Do shop around, however, Faith Stream, made in Australia, is a good option.

> *Enter through the narrow gate. For wide is the gate and broad is the road that leads to destruction, and many enter through it. But small is the gate and narrow the road that leads to life, and only a few find it...*   Matthew 7:13-14

How can I stay away from living in sin?

1. Cultivate a close relationship with God by reading and meditating on the Bible daily. Remind yourself regularly of the Ten Commandments and what God hates. Read Proverbs 6:16-19 and Mark 7:20-23. Remember and recite some of your favorite verses, including Psalm 119:9

2. Keep in step with the Holy Spirit. Read Galatians 5. Be careful what your eyes see and ears hear on a regular basis. Ask to be convicted of sin every day, so you can confess and repent. Learn to be content (Philippians 4:11-13)

3. Pray daily, also in tongues, if you have this spiritual

gift (1 Corinthians 14:18). Combine prayers with regular fasting, health permitting. Read Isaiah 58

4. Discern and be wise about who you spend time with, be accountable and part of a local church and Bible study group (Hebrews 3:12-14)

5. If you struggle in a particular area of sin, meet a trusted Christian friend or leader to discuss a time for healing and deliverance ministry

6. Ask God for a supple heart, receive Jesus' love, forgive those who sin against you, have love and care for others, give generously and keep your eyes fixed on Jesus

7. Useful websites: www.ellel.uk or www.healingrooms. org.uk

 Prayer

Dear Father in heaven, I thank You for standing with me during these trials of many kinds. I want to enter Your glory through the narrow gate which leads to eternal life. Please unveil my eyes and show me what offends You and what pleases You. Please forgive my sins and help me to make the necessary changes for Your glory alone. In Jesus' name, Amen.

CHAPTER 2

❧ SEPARATION ❧

The LORD said to Abram after Lot had parted from him, "Look around from where you are, to the north and south, to the east and west. All the land that you see I will give to you and your offspring forever.

GENESIS 13:14-15

Every person has done wrong and falls short of the glory of God (Romans 3:23). When we sin, this causes a separation from God and often from the person we wronged. Lot departed from Abraham but did he also separate from God for a short period? Separation from God can cause bondage and it is up to us to seek Him for our freedom. It is one thing to separate because you have too much possession which is crossing the boundary of another and causing confusion and argument, like Abraham and Lot, but it is another thing to not consult God before deciding where you will dwell thereafter. The consequences can be grave, even fatal. This should tell you before travelling, to research your destination. There are certain cities and countries which are no-go zones. If you go there, you travel at your own risk.

The once beautiful land of Sodom, was rich in minerals and produce. However, the condition of the hearts of those who lived there were far from pure.

If your close friend or relative told you they were going to Syria with their family, you may at first think they were not serious. If they then told you, it was for mission purposes to bring aid, your response may then be to advise them to leave their family behind for their own safety. Lot naturally took his family unaware of what dangers lay ahead.

No-one knows how Lot felt at this point. He may have had mixed emotions, as separation can produce a feeling of loneliness. All levels of society can feel lonely, from the road sweeper to the Prime Minister. One can feel forsaken just by having a mere opinion which is different to the majority. Sir Winston Churchill may have experienced this during his later premiership when Britain was at war against Germany. Just because you are the minority in your views, it does not mean you are wrong. Sir Winston Churchill's guts, wisdom, and genuine love for his people and country has enabled the UK to be what it is today. Germany was unable to take the UK through guns and fighting, it has not been able to take her through the European Union (EU), however, is there something else more subtle trying to steal her freedom? Those who continue to stand up and fight for freedom are finding themselves side-lined, cancelled and feeling quite isolated from the rest of the world.

Separation can bring pain and grief and we often ask why God allows the antagonism we currently see in the world? Today we notice nations rise up against nations, big techs against giant techs, groups against different groups, households against other households. We witnessed married couples being separated in queues outside supermarkets and other public places during COVID restrictions. This may seem relatively minor to some but to those who feel at one with their spouse, to be told off for talking or being next to your life-long partner at any particular time, verges on the demonic. The enemy hates togetherness as he himself was tossed out of heaven, thrown down to the pit of the earth, only to wage war, which he has already lost against his opponent, our Father in heaven, Luke 10:18. I quote, Dr Kynan Bridges who stated, *"There has to be separation to determine who is who"*. It might be that God is sifting the wheat from the chaff in this season, testing who will stand for Him and remain on His side during persecution.

And let us consider how we may spur one another on toward love and good deeds, not giving up meeting together, as some are in the habit of doing, but encouraging one another—and all the more as you see the Day approaching.   Hebrews 10:24-25

Places of worship had been shut down, which went against the Magna Carta and scriptures (Hebrews 10:25) and is leaving many people spiritually bankrupt around the world. The Church has been separated not by choice but scattered through the guidance of the world leaders.

Some governments forced church gatherings to cease during lockdown by sending law enforcement officers such as the police to arrest and fine church leaders. It made me yearn for a leader like Moses, who was sent by God to speak up for God's people, to tell Pharaoh, *"Let My people go, so they may worship Me..."* Exodus 7:16. I thank God for those twenty seven pastors in Scotland, who during lockdown, spoke up for the Church and against closure and won the battle in the courts[1]. The world is now in a season where it has to rely on technology like never before. With small sized as well as large churches closing its doors, we thank God the buildings are not the true Church but the people themselves are the hands and feet of Jesus Christ, who is the Head (Colossians 1:18). Soon the One-New-Man will unite together to be ready for the second coming, what the enemy meant for harm, God has turned for His good and the Gentile church has more opportunity to join forces with the Messianic believers around the world, as some believers worship whilst continuing to tune into services online.

The main concerns about online church however, are that many believers are losing the personal contact and accountability required as people of God. Also, when churches reopened, the congregations were not allowed to sing, stand up or dance to worship God, and everyone were to distance themselves from each other, except for immediate families. It appeared the State was running the churches in England and only a handful of church

1. www.christian.org.uk

leaders dared to contest this. The pain of loneliness, like never before set in due to feeling disconnected. Even I personally have cried many tears not only for myself but also for others, especially the vulnerable in society.

As the deer pants for streams of water,

so my soul pants for you, my God.

My soul thirsts for God, for the living God.

When can I go and meet with God?

My tears have been my food

day and night,

while people say to me all day long,

"Where is your God?"

These things I remember

as I pour out my soul:

how I used to go to the house of God

under the protection of the Mighty One

with shouts of joy and praise

among the festive throng.

Why, my soul, are you downcast?

Why so disturbed within me?

Put your hope in God,

for I will yet praise him,

my Savior and my God.   Psalm 42:1-5

The issue of a dependency on 'internet church' is this may leave the believers open to a one-world government dictatorship. Through Social Media platforms, a new law could be placed to stop and interrupt church services or manipulate what is shown and heard publicly. Also, those behind the anti-christ could appear without warning on your screens to preach propaganda, false doctrine and blaspheme the living God. As more believers become desperate to worship God in spirit and truth together, could this be a time when more underground churches will emerge by meeting in houses, so the Holy Spirit can continue to work through the Body of Christ freely, as it was originally in the book of Acts? There are stories in the Bible where some of God's people did not submit to the authority of their land, in order to not disobey God's law and teaching. Examples can be found in: Exodus 1:15-20; Esther 3:1-4; Daniel 3:18, 6:10; Acts 4:3, 17-20; 5:17-18, 28-29 and Galatians 1:10. Maybe this is a season when you will see the five-fold ministry come to life, so true believers will be seen as real disciples and fulfil the Great Commission as Jesus commanded in Matthew 28:18-20.

> *Then Jesus came to them and said, "All authority in heaven and on earth has been given to me. Therefore go and make disciples of all nations, baptizing them in the name of the Father and of the Son and of the Holy Spirit, and teaching them to obey everything I have commanded you. And surely I am with you always, to the very end of the age."*
>
> Matthew 28:18-20

In fact, everyone is susceptible to the 'big brother' approach, the super powers and globalists watching your every movement through the mobile phones, the backs of which you can no longer open to see what chip they may have fitted to spy on you. Some leaders want an excuse to bring in the 5G network, hungry for more power to control the people and make all individuals their subjects, similar to the current situation in China. Such leaders, plan to replace religion, especially Christianity and Judaism. They want to run everything by artificial intelligence (AI) and control everyone by drugs, do away with human interaction, replacing it by internal algorithms, and finally controlling personal income and expenditure. The idea is to have a world devoid of feeling, hope and love. We see a desperation for the unseen powers who must be obeyed, to take reign and even defy the living God by their wicked behavior and direct disobedience against His word (Romans 1:18-20).

During lockdown, places of recreation and leisure were taken away, adversely affecting our physical health. The first time in history, you are being told who you can and cannot meet outside and within your own homes; in fact, at one stage, you could not meet anyone except your spouse or family member living there. This was equivalent to house-arrest, taking away our civil liberties and causing mental illness. Some organisations have appointed Mental Health First Aiders as many employees reach mental melt-down under the strain and pressure of the current day. Laws of quarantine were not instigated by modern man until the seventeenth century. Almost 3,500 years back, the Bible tells the children of Israel what to do if a man has an infectious disease, plague or leprosy (Leviticus 13:46); as long as they had the disease, they remained unclean. They must live alone; they must live outside the camp. The lie today, is everyone could have a disease, whether it shows or not, so separation through social distancing or lockdown is justified.

Although some may argue the local and national lockdowns were God's reset on our lives and some have even benefited from the lockdowns happening all around the world, many would agree that lives have been frustrated, bound and some even destroyed. It makes you wonder how the Israelites may have felt when Pharaoh was slowly clamping down on their movement and causing them to do things they did not feel called to do. Similarly, how did the people who were stolen from Africa to become slaves in the West feel when they were separated and watched their freedom eroded and were ill-treated as though animals? How did the Jewish people feel when the Nazi regime, ordered by Hitler, instructed other people to spy and snitch on them, and to keep away from them? The Jewish people in Europe were hunted like animals, tortured and murdered in cold blood. These types of atrocities can only be described as sheer evil.

Fear and isolation have gripped individuals like never before, from the youngest to the oldest; from the lay person to the Minister. The Media did not help, by excessive bombarding of negative news across the globe.

The result of this, as already mentioned, is that more and more people are seeking God and joining churches online as services are led over the internet. However, sadly, some people have turned to other idols, including addiction to pornography, alcohol and drugs. The suicide rate has increased since lockdown and depression has set in where people are unable to deal with the uncertainty and drastic unprecedented changes.

Are we in the last days where Jesus said, "…the love of many will grow cold" (Matthew 24:12)? Are we expecting to witness further social distancing rules and other lockdown measures being enforced?

The time may be drawing nearer to the period Jesus referred to:

> *"Brother will betray brother to death, and a father his child. Children will rebel against their parents and have them put to death. Everyone will hate you because of me, but the one who stands firm to the end will be saved…"*   Mark 13:12-13

Those who are for freedom in Christ (Galatians 5:1), may be sold out by those who give in to slavery. Like the Israelites who wanted to return to Egypt because they had good things in Egypt but without true worship towards God, compare this with being in the dry desert, yet with God's powerful presence in your midst. Better is one day in the courts of the LORD than a thousand elsewhere (Psalm 84:10).

I had a dream a few years ago about lots of people in different communities in the UK, roaming around in the dark and misty night, walking in one direction to get out of their village. Everyone looked like they were in despair as they could not leave due to electronic barricades at the end of each street. There were uniformed guards wearing arm bands, walking around and telling people to return to their homes. It was an eerie feeling of totalitarianism and there was nothing anyone could do about it.

We all know about the recent protests in China, concerning their continued lockdown after all the other countries stopped theirs. Now we hear plans for climate change restrictions in at least two cities within the UK, being trialed and tested to prevent people travelling in their cars more than a certain number of times a year outside their zone because of the climate change theory. We also hear of the new climate ten commandments, which makes it appear as a new religion for people of all faiths to get involved.

No man, scientist, or secret agent can alter or fully understand the law and order of planet earth's rotation or the weather; only God, who made the entire universe can. Read Psalm chapter 19 and 2 Peter chapter 3 simultaneously. It is about time the people of the world stopped worshipping the 'world' and start worshipping the Word, which is Jesus Christ (John 1:1-2). So, look upon the One whom was pieced for our wrong-doing and created us for freedom in Him.

Many leaders of the world today view members of the population as unclean or rebellious, especially if you do not meet certain conditions or follow their narrative. For this and other reasons, there could be future lockdowns or restrictions on our God-given freedom, hence division from loved-ones. Regarding the Jewish woman who had been bleeding for more than twelve years without any doctors able to provide a cure (Mark 5:33), she would have understood separation in her time to the maximum degree. I again, quote Rabbi Jason Sobel, "This bleeding woman had been living in exile on all four levels. She had no physical contact with family and friends, could not publicly worship in the temple, was isolated and alone, and lived in a perpetual state of physical pain. But she found the fourfold healing by touching one of the four corners of Jesus' garment, and thus she became an example of the messianic redemption that we begin to experience right now when we reach out and touch Him!"

How can I stay together and connected with other people and Jesus?

1. If you attend a local church but do not yet know Jesus the Messiah or wish to return, reach out to Him through your believing family, friends or a leader in a church. Or you can simply say the short prayer of salvation in the Appendix: This will kick start the healing process within your soul, spirit and body. Read Zechariah 8:22-23 and Revelation 22

2. If you are a born-again believer, abide in Christ, pray for wisdom and resilience and seek God's counsel and guidance (everyone has different callings), John 15. Reach out to your immediate neighbours, snatch others from the fire (Jude 28-29). Be prepared to do 'underground church', like in the book of Acts and you will witness the power and glory of God. Do not conform to the patterns of this world but be transformed by the renewing of your mind (Romans 12:2)

3. Meet people you know in person, if you can. If online is your only option, ask someone to help you get started on Zoom or one of the safe social media or other communication platforms

4. Meet a trusted friend or family member on a regular basis for chats, fun and support. If possible, try to go for walks to see God's nature together and ponder on His beauty (Philippians 4:8-9)

5. If you have no friends and family, try connecting with Christian work colleagues, your local churches, house fellowships and support agencies. God showed Elijah he was not alone but God had preserved a remnant of seven thousand (1 Kings 19:18); also read 2 Kings 6:16-18 and Romans 8:31. Ask for deliverance from the spirit of fear, if you are living in constant bondage and are afraid to leave your home or be around other individuals. You may also benefit from reading my testimony on how I got free from chronic fear/

Post-Traumatic Stress Disorder (PTSD), in my book 'You Fit Perfectly'

6. Seek practical and legal advice. Ask what your rights are, especially as a living man or woman of the land. Do your research about how Common Law may protect you, your household, job or business

7. Useful websites and Telephone numbers: www. christianhelpline. uk – Tel: 0808 801 0585; www.ucb. co.uk/pray - Tel: 01782 36 3000; www.samaritans. org – Tel: 116 123; www.relate.org.uk; www. bereavementadvice.org; - Tel: 0800 634 9494; www. commonlawcourt.com; www.christianconcern.com – Tel: 020 3327 1120

 Prayer

> *Dear Father in heaven, I thank You for standing with arms open wide for me to come to You. I thank You for not seeing me as unclean or unworthy because I chose to believe in You. I reach out to you now, please bring healing to my soul, body and spirit now? Just like you foreknew the enslavement of Your people for 400 years and You prepared a great deliverance (Genesis 14), You knew about today's diseases and corrupt schemes which bring restrictions that may occur in the future and what greater deliverance is coming, even the return of the LORD Jesus Himself. Only You know the exact time. I surrender to You*

Abba (Father), knowing the reason you allow Your people to be in bondage is always to show the world and remind Your children that You are ADONAI, creator God, who is all knowing, all powerful and present everywhere. No-one can topple You off of Your Throne! I put my hope and trust in You and not my own understanding, knowing You will come back for me at the appointed time and take me to a place where I will never experience separation or loneliness ever again! In Jesus' name, Amen.

CHAPTER 3

❧ SEEKING RESCUE ❧

*Then the king of Sodom, the king of Gomorrah, the king
of Admah, the king of Zeboyim and the king of Bela
(that is, Zoar) marched out and drew up their battle
lines in the Valley of Siddim against Kedorlaomer king
of Elam, Tidal king of Goyim, Amraphel king of Shinar
and Arioch king of Ellasar—four kings against five.
Now the Valley of Siddim was full of tar pits, and when
the kings of Sodom and Gomorrah fled, some of the
men fell into them and the rest fled to the hills. The four
kings seized all the goods of Sodom and Gomorrah and
all their food; then they went away. They also carried
off Abram's nephew Lot and his possessions, since he
was living in Sodom.
A man who had escaped came and reported this to
Abram the Hebrew. Now Abram was living near the
great trees of Mamre the Amorite, a brother of Eshkol
and Aner, all of whom were allied with Abram. When
Abram heard that his relative had been taken captive,
he called out the 318 trained men born in his household
and went in pursuit as far as Dan. During the night
Abram divided his men to attack them and he routed
them, pursuing them as far as Hobah, north of Da-*

mascus. He recovered all the goods and brought back his relative Lot and his possessions, together with the women and the other people.

Genesis 14:8-16

When we are lost or in a dark and difficult place, we all need rescuing. What situation are you in today? What is your Sodom and Gomorrah? We can often look back after making mistakes and wonder how we got into this spot. Lot may have felt even more isolated to think that his own men argued with men of a righteous and peaceable man like Abraham, and suddenly have to put things into perspective as to who to pick his fights with. In view of this, I wonder how many quarrels over wealth took place in Sodom?

What was in Sodom during Lot's days? Sodom was a place where, although it may have looked beautiful with much wealth, a person who wanted to please God would have felt extremely isolated. That righteous person could only live there by the grace of God.

We find ourselves living in towns, villages, cities and nations full of worldly behaviours which proves the majority of mankind has pushed God out of their equation. Preachers are arrested on the streets for preaching God's Gospel of peace, Christians are getting unfairly dismissed from their jobs for stating their God-fearing views on their own social media platforms, churches are becoming state-run, being told what they can and cannot do, hence prohibiting true and free worship to the God of Abraham, Isaac, and Jacob (Israel). This is happening whilst the teaching of same sex marriage, changing from a boy to a girl and vice versa are in schools and the UK are planning to teach children as young as six years of age, how to masturbate. Is this not child abuse? Abortion is at its highest rate and euthanasia is a hot debate.

As you know, sin is sin, so why then did God want to destroy Sodom? The way to find out is to research what God despises. God cannot stand pride, greed, wrath, envy, lust, gluttony, and sloth, which are contrary to the seven heavenly virtues which are, prudence, justice, temperance, courage, faith, hope and charity.

There are six things the LORD hates,
  seven that are detestable to him:
    haughty eyes,
    a lying tongue,
    hands that shed innocent blood,
    a heart that devises wicked schemes,
    feet that are quick to rush into evil,
    a false witness who pours out lies
    and a person who stirs up conflict in the
  community. Proverbs 6:16-19

Despite, all of the ungodly attitudes and actions we see in our world back then and today, the main reason why I believe God's wrath burned so strongly against

Sodom, that He decided to extinguish it, was due to man wanting to be in the place of God Himself. This was Lucifer's evil desire from the beginning, hence why he was cast out of the glory of God and renamed Satan. Pride was the root cause for Satan's envy, lust, lying, wicked schemes and evil which produced the mess we see today. Think about it, back in Noah's day, you see it written about man's disobedience to God and angels having sex with women to produce superhumans who were known as giants. See Genesis 6:4.

> When human beings began to increase in number
> on the earth and daughters were born to them,
> the sons of God saw that the daughters of humans
> were beautiful, and they married any of them they
> chose. Then the LORD said, "My Spirit will not
> contend with humans forever, for they are mortal;
> their days will be a hundred and twenty years."
> The Nephilim were on the earth in those days—and
> also afterward—when the sons of God went to the
> daughters of humans and had children by them. They
> were the heroes of old, men of renown. The LORD
> saw how great the wickedness of the human race
> had become on the earth, and that every inclination
> of the thoughts of the human heart was only evil
> all the time. The LORD regretted that he had made
> human beings on the earth, and his heart was deeply
> troubled. So the LORD said, "I will wipe from the
> face of the earth the human race I have created—and
> with them the animals, the birds and the creatures

*that move along the ground—for I regret that I have
made them." But Noah found favor in the eyes of the
LORD.*   Genesis 6:1-8

Similarly, the Tower of Babel caused God such concern to not only exterminate the city but to scatter the
people far and wide from each other and confuse their
communication (Genesis 11:1-9). Herod loved the people
worshipping him as a god instead of giving glory to God
and worms ate his heart so he died instantly (Acts 12:23).
In Sodom, men who were possessed with demons were
dominating other people, so as to take their God-given
freedom, space, dignity and peace away. They showed
irreverence towards God by wanting absolute and total
control, even malevolent rulership over the angels of
God (Genesis 19:5). So, as you can see, man today may
form groups which make decisions designed to control
the world, however, there is a judgement for every un-
confessed sin and behaviour which God clearly detests.
No-one can escape God's wrath, except those He has
saved for Himself, known as His remnant, like His friend
Abraham who, as we shall see in later chapters, interceded for the righteous people in Sodom and Gomorrah.

*The wrath of God is being revealed from heaven
against all the godlessness and wickedness of people,
who suppress the truth by their wickedness, since
what may be known about God is plain to them,
because God has made it plain to them. For since the
creation of the world God's invisible qualities—his
eternal power and divine nature—have been clearly*

seen, being understood from what has been made, so that people are without excuse. For although they knew God, they neither glorified him as God nor gave thanks to him, but their thinking became futile and their foolish hearts were darkened. Although they claimed to be wise, they became fools and exchanged the glory of the immortal God for images made to look like a mortal human being and birds and animals and reptiles. Therefore God gave them over in the sinful desires of their hearts to sexual impurity for the degrading of their bodies with one another. They exchanged the truth about God for a lie, and worshiped and served created things rather than the Creator—who is forever praised. Amen. Because of this, God gave them over to shameful lusts. Even their women exchanged natural sexual relations for unnatural ones. In the same way the men also abandoned natural relations with women and were inflamed with lust for one another. Men committed shameful acts with other men, and received in themselves the due penalty for their error. Furthermore, just as they did not think it worthwhile to retain the knowledge of God, so God gave them over to a depraved mind, so that they do what ought not to be done. They have become filled with every kind of wickedness, evil, greed and depravity. They are full of envy, murder, strife, deceit and malice. They are gossips, slanderers, God-haters, insolent, arrogant and boastful; they invent ways of doing evil; they disobey their parents; they have

no understanding, no fidelity, no love, no mercy.
Although they know God's righteous decree that
those who do such things deserve death, they not only
continue to do these very things but also approve of
those who practice them.   Romans 1:18-32

The name Sodom has various meanings in Hebrew such as division, burnt or demons, whilst Gomorrah means deep waters. No wonder there was always a sense of war and calamity. What righteous person would not long to be rescued from deep waters and demons?

Lot and his household, through no fault of their own, became victims of war. One could also argue that Lot's wealth made him a target and he was kidnapped as a result of rebellion. Those who felt they had been treated unjustly, saw Lot and his possessions as 'pay back' time. They may have thought Lot was among the wicked in the land, when all he was after was a quiet life with a land to grow his herd. This war may have come out of pride and anger towards Sodom and Gomorrah. And who ever lived there would be hit indiscriminately by the venom of the attackers.

Are we in the part of this era where Jesus said, *"nation will rise against nation"?* (Matthew 24:7). Russia were at one point accusing the UK and the West of deliberately infecting the world with the coronavirus, whilst Iran was accusing Israel of the same. Certain states in America are threatening China with a law suit. Can you see confusion and fear escalating to the point of the threat of a nuclear war? Certainly, a cyber war has already begun with Israel being hit. Russia is currently at war with Ukraine and any country who sides with Ukraine. There is growing tension between China and USA. There are civil battles and genocide within other countries, including Islamic terrorists murdering Christians in Nigeria and other parts of the world. Whatever the case, I believe God is showing His people something by way of a warning and preparing you for a personal revival, as the LORD continues to tear down the idols in your life. Read Isaiah 19, 2 Kings 23:24, Jerimiah 3, 2 Kings 23:24 and 2 Chronicles 34:33.

Lot and all his possessions were stolen by Sodom's enemies. How do you think Lot was feeling during this time of captivity? Here we have a real indication as to whether Lot had a relationship with God. He may have asked himself questions like, 'will I be used as their slaves, so they can make riches for themselves?' Or 'will they kill me and take all that is mine?' All Lot's livelihood and security, gone in seconds, just like Job. See the book of Job chapters 1 to 2. Job was a righteous man whom God allowed Satan to test by causing calamity in his life, whereby he lost all his children and possessions at the same time. This would have been a very lonely time for Job, especially as he was surrounded by loved-ones who failed to see what good God was trying to do through Job, in order to bring more glory to God.

Lot may have wondered whether he would have been better off nearer Abraham. He would have missed his uncle and realised his mistake in not fully respecting Abraham in the past. When you remove yourself from Godly protection due to lustful desires, you may reminisce about the virtue of the very things which drove you away in the first place. This would have been very humbling for Lot and his character would have been molded at this point. He may have had regrets about moving to Sodom and glad to see the back of it.

Although we are not always certain why calamity can suddenly come upon us, could your way of life and your actions have brought this on you? (Jerimiah 4:18). Hold the things of this world lightly. Get ready to be removed from your comfort zone.

> Many are the plans in a person's heart, but it is the
> LORD's plans that prevail.   Proverbs 19:21

Can you think of anything happening in the world today which might be similar to what happened in Sodom? Reflect for a moment and pray for the innocent victims and for the LORD to touch the heart of the perpetrators. Most importantly, if like Lot, you are in a place, where you need rescuing from either physical danger or from your own sins, cry out to God to save you.

How can I help rescue others?

1. Do spiritual warfare. Read and pray the scripture verses in Ephesians 6:10-18

2. Intercede for the protection and rescue of loved-ones, brothers and sisters in Christ around the world. Psalm 91:14-16

3. Ask God to raise up more labourers in the harvest field. Luke 10:2

4. Help build up the Body of Christ by discipling or mentoring another believer of the same gender. Ephesians 4:11-16. Resources can be found at: www.etsministries.org.uk

5. Choose to please God and not man by speaking the truth in love and speak up for those who cannot speak for themselves. Read Proverbs 31:8-9 and Esther chapters 3 to 5. Prayerfully consider supporting a Christian ministry which is rooted in scriptures and God's moral order

 Prayer

> *Dear Father, thank You for helping me to acknowledge that even I, myself, may not be in a good place, or have loved the world for all its ungodly trappings. I ask You to deliver me and my loved-ones? In Jesus name. Amen.*

Chapter 4

❧ Produce Fruit in Keeping with Repentance within our Sodom-like Culture ❧

The king of Sodom said to Abram, "Give me the people and keep the goods for yourself."
But Abram said to the king of Sodom, "With raised hand I have sworn an oath to the LORD, God Most High, Creator of heaven and earth, that I will accept nothing belonging to you, not even a thread or the strap of a sandal, so that you will never be able to say, 'I made Abram rich.'

Genesis 14:21-23

D o not just say, "I go to church, therefore I must be safe". John the Baptist spoke sternly to the Jewish leaders of his day to warn them of complacency in Matthew 3:8. The Bible says, a prudent man sees disaster coming and prepares his household for it, Proverbs 22:3. Abraham had a pure heart and was a true servant leader. His life was full of 'follow me' by example. He refused to be bought by Sodom but to remain set apart as holy. Abraham turned his heart from the so-called wealth of this world and chose to trust only God's divine provision for his life and future. Lot would more than likely have been Abraham's disciple as well as a type of son figure when they were close friends. Abraham's actions here, were purely out of principle to save his nephew, whatever the cost and for no fee. Abraham's brave actions could have cost him his life but he expressed his love for a friend and showed the heart of Jesus Christ, who forgave our sins and rescued us from the pit of hell.

Where can you find leaders like Abraham today? Such Godly influential people are few and far between. Most people who govern, tend to lord it over the people they rule with harshness, while some abuse their positions out of greed, by lying and accepting bribes to gain more power and fame. Most people in the UK are concerned about how they will pay three times their current energy bills, if the fuel suppliers, who are already making millions of profits, have their way. However, the Church must show itself as different, or we run the risk of being likened to the lukewarm hypocritical church of Laodicia, where Jesus said, He will spew them out of His mouth. See Revelation 3:15-17.

The Prophet Micah was another example of a righteous leader, who loved justice and warned the people about their wrong, greed, wickedness and God's judgement. This brings me to my next point, which is to question the type of leadership in Sodom and Gomorrah. For anarchy to exist in a city or nation, their leaders must give an account.

This is what the LORD says:

"As for the prophets
  who lead my people astray,
they proclaim 'peace'
  if they have something to eat,
but prepare to wage war against anyone
  who refuses to feed them.
Therefore night will come over you, without visions,
  and darkness, without divination.
The sun will set for the prophets,
  and the day will go dark for them.
The seers will be ashamed
  and the diviners disgraced.
They will all cover their faces
  because there is no answer from God."
But as for me, I am filled with power,
  with the Spirit of the LORD,
  and with justice and might,
to declare to Jacob his transgression,
  to Israel his sin.
Hear this, you leaders of Jacob,
  you rulers of Israel,
who despise justice
  and distort all that is right;
who build Zion with bloodshed,
  and Jerusalem with wickedness.
Her leaders judge for a bribe,
  her priests teach for a price,
  and her prophets tell fortunes for money.
Yet they look for the LORD's support and say,
  "Is not the LORD among us?

No disaster will come upon us."
Therefore because of you,
*   Zion will be plowed like a field,*
Jerusalem will become a heap of rubble,
*   the temple hill a mound overgrown with thickets.*
Micah 3:5-12

Righteous leaders produce good fruit and are consistent in their direction. Lot would have been reminded that God was truly on Abraham's side, offering him special protection and Lot may have become even more humbled and got his life right with God at this stage.

After Abraham brought Lot and his family back to Sodom, Lot, after having the chance to reminisce, may have repented of his treatment towards Abraham. Who knows, maybe Lot was in a state of further shock to find himself back from where he came. As a dog returns to his vomit, so a fool returns to his folly (Proverbs 26:11).

This was Lot's chance to say to Abraham, 'you were right and I was wrong in my quarrel against you. Now I choose not to stay in this wicked city but return, to be nearer to you or go somewhere else where the people fear the God of Abraham.'

Lot may have felt lonelier at the thought of returning to a city where he knew he did not fit spiritually, and may have been struggling to leave Sodom due to his connections which kept him wealthy. Nevertheless, Lot had a chance at this stage to escape Sodom but did not.

There are lots of reasons why we, today, chose to remain in a place similar to Sodom, especially when you look around the world and see corruption in every nation.

God's people over the years have had many chances to leave Sodom. Sodom can be a type of mindset which you do not want to change, no matter the cost. Greed, power, lust, selfish ambition and complacency can keep you tied to this type of world God did not intend for us to be in. However, the main reason Lot was left in Sodom was to show God's glory. Lot on this occasion would understand he was set apart and would have started to produce fruit in keeping with repentance, Matthew 3:8. We will later on, see that Lot did some things which showed he had really given up his sins.

It is good to think of the Exodus, when God prepared His people for the great deliverance from Egypt. The Israelites had a free-will to disobey God but they all went along with God's orders through Moses and experienced the LORD's mighty miracles in parting the Red Sea and eating Manna from heaven. It was in the wilderness where God's people sinned as they forgot His covenant, miraculous power and great provision. They also forgot God's mighty protection over their families and loved ones, especially when God preserved their first-born sons. Only few can imagine the pain of losing your first-born child, which is a million times greater than the boils, blood rivers, locusts, frogs and hail stones. Such grief would last a lifetime.

Back to the UK and the rest of the world today, March 2020 brought everyone into a state of shock due to the variants of coronavirus. The world after years of leadership suppression will never be the same again. As mentioned previously, pubs, theatres, cinemas, national galleries, heritage, clubs, schools and restaurants were forced to close and those people who could retain their jobs following mass redundancies, were told to work from home. Keeping away from each other and wearing PPE equipment made the world look like it had either gone mad or was in a completely different era. Anyone outside of this were excluded from what would be deemed as 'normal society'. Individuals were being trained to think this ought to be the norm. With many high street shops going out of business, internet shopping had become compulsory for some, digitally excluding many of the elderly, poor and disabled who had to depend on friends, family or support workers from a controlled agency to help them survive.

Parts of the USA have food shortages and energy prices are hiked up all over the globe. Rumours of recessions and a global financial crash has caused more people to panic buy in stores as people stock up for an uncertain future and time of hibernation. Anarchy is on the increase around the world with even more able-bodied people afraid to leave their homes. This could justify the army being deployed to work with the police and other law enforcements on the streets, never to be the same.

Freedom as we know it could be eroded and the so-called antidote to be given in order to cure or stop future pandemics may, if the prophesies are true, be more lethal than the pestilence itself. Who can you trust in these last days? Everything is happening so fast; no-one could have predicted the past year's events. This is a wake-up call from God for His chosen people to arise, put on His full armour and do battle alongside Him in the heavenlies as we intercede for God's people and the returning of the LORD. Remember, Christ already has the victory! It is a done deal.

Could this be a time of judgement with a small 'j'? Sodom and Gomorrah were also a type of judgement and I believe we are currently living in more evil days. I believe God is trying to get the world's attention in this time of awakening; trying to cause everyone to look upwards, rather than rely of ourselves. It may be difficult for many people but God is peeling away layer by layer, like an onion. The key is true repentance.

And you, Capernaum, will you be lifted to the heavens? No, you will go down to Hades. For if the miracles that were performed in you had been performed in Sodom, it would have remained to this day. Matthew 11:23

In relation to the Exodus, all of His chosen people were obedient and even some Egyptians, who learnt the fear of God, followed suit. Think of the blood of the lamb on their door posts, symbolising their union with God and divine protection. You are not of this world but still in it until our LORD returns. This means as the children of God, you will be caught in the cross fire of Satan's battle with God's Kingdom. Lot was trapped in this same old ancient battle, manifested in a way where all of the population of Sodom but a few were possessed with the devil. Just like God devised a plan to protect the Israelites in Egypt, He had a strategy to save Lot and his family. This should assure you that God also has a plot to deliver you, who are truly repentant, from the present Sodom you find yourself in today.

Watch out for false prophets. They come to you in sheep's clothing, but inwardly they are ferocious wolves. By their fruit you will recognize them. Do people pick grapes from thornbushes, or figs from thistles? Likewise, every good tree bears good fruit, but a bad tree bears bad fruit. A good tree cannot bear bad fruit, and a bad tree cannot bear good fruit. Every tree that does not bear good fruit is cut down and thrown into the fire. Thus, by their fruit you will recognize them. Matthew 7:15-20

How do I produce good fruit?

1. Keep a pure heart and clean hands. Psalm 24:3. Keep on confessing and repenting with Godly sorrow, 2 Corinthians 7:10. Having a supple heart, includes walking in love and forgiveness towards others and doing things which keep you humble. 1 Peter 5:6 & 2 Chronicles 7:14

2. Read the book of Jude in the Bible or in the appendix of this book. Ask God to show you your purpose on earth

3. Give out free Bibles, including New Testaments to as many unbelievers as possible (you may wish to join your local Good News for Everyone branch)

4. Exhibit the Fruit of the Holy Spirit in your daily life. Read Galatians 5:22-23 & Isaiah 58:6-14

5. Let your life be a witness, Matthew 5:16.

 Prayer

Dear Heavenly Father, thank You for being close to me when I need You and even when I think I do not. I understand Your anger towards this generation, O how we have gone astray, so far that we now have a big elephant in the room we cannot see. I repent for my part in this mess. I specifically repent of ... (name them). Please help me to produce good fruit that will last for Your glory. In Jesus' name. Amen.

CHAPTER 5

❧ CHRIST OUR MEDIATOR IN HEAVEN ❧

Then he said, "May the LORD not be angry,
but let me speak just once more.
What if only ten can be found there?"
He answered, "For the sake of ten,
I will not destroy it."

GENESIS 18:32

The two angels arrived at Sodom in the evening, and
Lot was sitting in the gateway of the city. When he saw
them, he got up to meet them and bowed down with his
face to the ground.

GENESIS 19:1

braham was a type of Jesus Christ interceding for His Bride (the Church) left on earth which is, a type of Sodom, John 17:6-26 and Hebrews 7:25. Jesus knows those who are His and is praying for us now, pleading with God our Father on our behalf. Jesus, Himself knows what it is like to be tempted and has love and compassion for us, Hebrews 4:16.

Everyone has a moral conscience and knows the boundaries in which they can tolerate changes in society which tear down traditional family values. There is a limit to moral conduct when we have to say, enough is enough. This is not even about judging others because God is the only just Judge. It is about going with your strong principles and asking yourself, can you live in a society where pedophilia has been legalised, so it may seem 'normal'? Where a government says it is no longer a crime for an adult to have sexual intercourse with animals and children, including babies – is this something you can stomach? I know full well, I cannot. How about a society where they make it legal to kill babies up to a month after they come out of the womb? Is this not murder in cold blood? Surely this is child sacrifice which God forbids in His word (Leviticus 18:21). Well, as distressing and disturbing as it sounds, these are subjects which we learn are actually happening or on the discussion tables of some groups and governments around the world.

Let us do the maths:

Lot plus (+) Lot's wife plus (+) two daughters plus (+) two son-in-laws, equals (=) six people.

Therefore,

Six people minus (–) two son-in-laws, who actually thought Lot was joking (Genesis 19:14), equals (=) four people.

These four escaped Sodom to endeavour to reach

safe humble soil, Genesis 19:20-22. However, in the process, Lot's wife disobeyed God and looked back, equals (=) three survivors only.

So, in God's eyes, only three people were righteous in Sodom and Gomorrah, that is, one adult man and two young virgin women. This very fact makes me weep tears of sorrow over the souls in the world we find ourselves in today. How many will God find faithful when He returns? Lot had repented and turned to God by this stage. This point is proven when Lot bowed down to God and called the angels 'my LORD' (Genesis 19: 1).

"...My LORDs," he said, "please turn aside to your servant's house. You can wash your feet and spend the night and then go on your way early in the morning."

"No," they answered, "we will spend the night in the square."

But he insisted so strongly that they did go with him and entered his house. He prepared a meal for them, baking bread without yeast, and they ate. Before they had gone to bed, all the men from every part of the city of Sodom—both young and old—surrounded the house. They called to Lot, "Where are the men who came to you tonight? Bring them out to us so that we can have sex with them." Lot went outside to meet them and shut the door behind him and said, "No, my friends. Don't do this wicked thing. Look, I have

*two daughters who have never slept with a man. Let
me bring them out to you, and you can do what you
like with them. But don't do anything to these men,
for they have come under the protection of my roof."*

Genesis 19: 2-8

God honoured His word to Abraham, because three
being less than ten meant God had to destroy Sodom
but in His infinite mercy, due to Abraham's prayers of
intercession, snatched only four righteous people away
from His wrath (Genesis 18:32). Abraham interceded
for Sodom and Gomorrah as a prophet, and we ought
to do likewise, when God shows us, calamity is about
to come upon a city, nation or the world. Abraham had
invested interest in the land of Sodom and Gomorrah
and was sure his sound teaching to Lot, while he was
young, would have produced a fruit of righteousness.
This confirms why it is crucial for the older generation to
teach the younger God's law. We can see an example in
scripture where Ezra was told to teach people how to be
God-fearing (Ezra 7:25). Likewise, Jesus commanded His
disciples to teach all future disciples to obey everything
He taught. Hence, why discipleship training is para-
mount today and something, God willing, Equipping
the Saints (ETS) Ministries will continue to teach until
Jesus returns. Read Matthew 28:18-20.

*People were eating, drinking, marrying and being
given in marriage up to the day Noah entered the ark.
Then the flood came and destroyed them all.*

Luke 17:27

So, what does it mean to be set apart? To show true repentance today is to humble yourself and put your trust in our LORD Jesus Christ who exchanged our sin with His righteousness. It is only through Christ's righteousness that you can be saved from the wrath of God that is about to come upon the nations like you have never seen before since time began. Noah was seen as righteous in God's eyes and was rescued by God before God showed His wrath on mankind, Genesis 6:9. Lot was also delivered in Genesis 19:22, and so should the saints who are on earth during the church age, expect to be removed and taken to a place of safety, in Jesus' arms, before the soon coming wrath in the Tribulation, as Ephesians 1:13 states:

And you also were included in Christ when you heard the message of truth, the gospel of your salvation. When you believed, you were marked in him with a seal, the promised Holy Spirit, who is a deposit guaranteeing our inheritance until the redemption of those who are God's possession—to the praise of his glory.

It is unclear whether Lot sat at the gateway of the city as Sodom's ruling council, where legal matters were discussed or whether he literally sat at the gate alone. The gateway can be a solemn place for someone to wait when you are contemplating leaving. It could almost be perceived as 'sitting on the fence'. Indecision could cause hesitation, which could cause death when disaster is knocking on your door. We have all done this at least once in our lives. Being indecisive can be frustrating and you could end up feeling like you are chasing your own tail. Read James 1:8.

How many times have you needed to make a decisive decision which affects not just you but your loved ones? Have you had strong views about situations happening around you, which are in opposition to the majority, including those within your household? Instead of sitting on the fence, get on the right side, that which lines up with God's will. Lot may have been in arguments with his family about the state of Sodom & Gomorrah, which may have exacerbated his feeling of loneliness.

The UK went through a similar experience when families, friends, neighbors, colleagues and even the church split on BREXIT, and most recently over how CORONAVIRUS lockdown measures ought to be handled. Sometimes people just want to escape the strife. Could Lot at this time have been researching the small town next to Sodom, praying to God about humbling himself by downsizing? After all, better poor in peace and quiet than being wealthy but full of strife (Proverbs 17:1).

One thing we do know is that Lot, by this stage, chose to distinguish himself from the people of Sodom. Lot was clearly set apart by God and this was evidenced by Lot refusing to engage in the foul behavior of the people of Sodom.

How to intercede for the nations and offer practical help?

1. Start small and pray from your home – use The LORD's prayer as a guide, Luke 11:1-4. I quote D.L Moody: *"Every great movement of God can be traced to a kneeling figure"*

2. Ask the Holy Spirit to help you align your prayers with God's heart and use scriptures, Exodus 17:8-13

3. Pray for more love and compassion and for the salvation of the unsaved

4. Research the persecuted churches around the world and pray for your brothers and sisters. Subscribe to Heart Publications, which is a free Christian newspaper (www.heartpublications.co.uk)

5. Join your local church prayer team or pray for and serve in your local community, with small Christian groups

6. Join the Prayer Shield network and Prayer for Israel (PfI). Romans 10:1. https://theprayershield.uk and https://prayerforisrael.org

7. Get active in evangelism and discipleship, Matthew 28:18-20. Equipping the Saints (ETS) Ministries based in UK provide practical training and Discipleship Manuals to reach more souls and help

build up the Body of Christ. You can find out more at: www.etsministries.org.uk

 Prayer

Dear God, thank You for Jesus Christ, my Mediator. I know You have a plan to deliver me from this corrupt world. Please help me to intervene practically where I can, so others, especially my loved-ones can also be saved? Use me for Your glory. In Jesus' name. Amen.

CHAPTER 6

❧ LOOKING BACK BEFORE THE RAPTURE ❧

As soon as they had brought them out,
one of them said, "Flee for your lives! Don't look back,
and don't stop anywhere in the plain! Flee to the moun-
tains or you will be swept away!" ...By the time Lot
reached Zoar, the sun had risen over the land.
Then the LORD rained down burning sulfur on Sodom
and Gomorrah—from the LORD out of the heavens.
Thus he overthrew those cities and the entire plain,
destroying all those living in the cities—and also the
vegetation in the land. But Lot's wife looked back, and
she became a pillar of salt.

Genesis 19:17; 23-26

What is the point of living if you are sleeping all day? Many lonely people who fall into depression, end up physically asleep during the day time. But some others who are regularly active, are spiritually unawake to what is actually happening, which makes them wonder why they sense deep seclusion. There are many Christians who are numb and not ready, like the five women in the Parable of the Wise and Foolish Virgins, Matthew

25:1-4. Could this parable reflect the condition of the churches today? Half the Church prepared by ensuring they carry God's anointing and the other half complacent and worldly, to the extent that when they eventually wake up, it may be too late to be raptured, hence, they will have to go through the Tribulation with unbelieving Israel.

If today's Israeli leaders, know how to prepare their people for a war crisis, rather than a cost-of-living crisis, why cannot the church leaders concoct a plan for Christ's soldiers to be ready for the big spiritual battle ahead? Even soldiers get ready for battle, and does not a bride prepare for her groom? Of course, like Queen Esther bathed and perfumed herself daily, the Body of Christ should and must be excited as we prepare ourselves to be sweet-smelling and spotless for when our heavenly King and Groom comes to snatch us up to be with Him forever! Read Ephesians 5:27.

Like Lot's wife, I pray you will not become a pillar of salt. Reflecting on your past can be a good thing, if you use it to figure out your present state and plan your Godly future. However, in certain situations, the consequences of looking back can be grave, like those Israelites who, after the Exodus, despised the manna from heaven, looked back and longed to return to Egypt where they were slaves and were unable to properly worship the One true God. Just like Lot could not take any of his possessions with him, neither can you when your redemption comes. It is advisable for us all to do a heart MOT on a regular basis.

What is the condition of your heart today? Jesus said, *"For where your treasure is, there your heart will be also"*, Matthew 6:21. This takes us back to the first and greatest commandment, back in chapter one, where we looked at sinning against God by having idols in your life. Are you caught up with your nice family, house, car, possessions, career, medical service, prime minister, king or queen? Have you got a few gods in your life? Just because you are not paying homage by physically bowing down to them, it does not mean you are not worshipping them. Are you ungrateful for the costly price Jesus paid for you? As God's chosen, you are merely passing through this earth, which itself is decaying. Your true citizenship is in heaven. No eye has seen, no ear has heard what God has in store for those who love Him, 1 Corinthians 2:9. Check your heart for purity. 1 John 3:2-3 states:

> *Dear friends, now we are children of God, and what we will be has not yet been made known. But we know that when Christ appears, we shall be like him, for we shall see him as he is. All who have this hope in him purify themselves, just as he is pure.*

There are better things for us in the Promised Land, the new heaven and earth Jesus promised us. Part of this promise is peace and security, no more pain, sorrow, death and evil, Revelation 21. Our heavenly prize is what we ought to fix our gaze on. The Apostle John wrote, *"Do not love the world or anything in the world. If anyone loves the world, love for the Father is not in them. For everything in the world—the lust of the flesh, the lust of the eyes, and the pride of life—comes not from the Father but from the world. The world and its desires pass away, but whoever does the will of God lives forever." 1 John 2:15-17.*

When your focus is too much on the things of this world, it becomes a distraction from the things of God. Although God made planet earth and saw it was good originally, He wants you to remember the current state is fallen due to sin. And only through His Son Jesus Christ, do we have redemption. Therefore, we need to put God alone on the throne of our hearts. His desire for us is to give us, believers, a new beginning where this earth will pass away and a new heaven and earth will be joined, so He can live with us and we, in Him. If we are led astray by the world, we may not be ready for our time of deliverance (otherwise known as The Rapture) from the present day 'Sodom'. We are only righteous because of God's grace through our faith in Him and what the LORD has done on the Cross for us. God, the Father, is getting ready to give the nod for when His Son, Jesus Christ, is to return to earth to sweep up His spotless Bride. If you are feeling like an alien, like the five awake virgins, then you are not alone. Bearing in mind, Lot may have felt like the only remaining dinosaur on earth, what incredible relief and joy he would have experienced after heeding the LORD's warning to escape not just the fire and brimstone, but the vile behaviour of his friends and community, and look towards his heavenly prize. Therefore, Lot being taken out of Sodom, is synonymous with the Church being raptured.

> *Blessed is he who reads and those who hear the words*
> *of this prophecy, and keep those things which are*
> *written in it; for the time is near.*
>
> Revelation 1:3

The Book of Revelation, interestingly enough, means 'unveiling', and makes it clear there is a limit on the time available on earth. God promises an eternal life of heaven for those who accept Jesus as Messiah. Although there are three different debates about whether Jesus will return for His church before, during or after the seven-year Tribulation, the early church believed Jesus will first return privately for His Bride, without actually stepping on earth. This triggers the seven-year Tribulation, which is imminent. Then publicly, sometime after seven years, at the second coming, He steps on earth at the Mount of Olives to execute judgement. I believe this particular argument, that is, the church being caught up with Christ will occur just prior to the seven-year Tribulation, because Jacob's Trouble (which is another name given to the seven-year Tribulation) is primarily designed as judgement on the unbelieving Jewish community, so the last remnant will be saved before Christ's Millennium reign on earth. A few scriptures which support this is found in the book of Revelation, where those seven churches represent the End Time churches today, and various other places in the Bible.

Then I will return to my lair
until they have borne their guilt
and seek my face—
in their misery
they will earnestly seek me.   Hosea 5:15

With praise and thanksgiving they sang to the
LORD:
"He is good;
his love toward Israel endures forever."
Ezra 3:11a

Be always on the watch, and pray that you may be
able to escape all that is about to happen, and that
you may be able to stand before the Son of Man.
Luke 21:36

Since you have kept my command to endure
patiently, I will also keep you from the hour of trial
that is going to come on the whole world to test the
inhabitants of the earth.   Revelation 3:10

Listen, I tell you a mystery: We will not all sleep, but
we will all be changed— in a flash, in the twinkling
of an eye, at the last trumpet. For the trumpet
will sound, the dead will be raised imperishable,
and we will be changed. For the perishable must
clothe itself with the imperishable, and the mortal
with immortality. When the perishable has been
clothed with the imperishable, and the mortal
with immortality, then the saying that is written

will come true: "Death has been swallowed up in victory."

"Where, O death, is your victory

Where, O death, is your sting?"
1 Corinthians 15:51-55

Concerning the coming of our LORD Jesus Christ and our being gathered to him, we ask you, brothers and sisters, not to become easily unsettled or alarmed by the teaching allegedly from us—whether by a prophecy or by word of mouth or by letter—asserting that the day of the LORD has already come. Don't let anyone deceive you in any way, for that day will not come until the rebellion occurs and the man of lawlessness is revealed, the man doomed to destruction. He will oppose and will exalt himself over everything that is called God or is worshiped, so that he sets himself up in God's temple, proclaiming himself to be God.

Don't you remember that when I was with you I used to tell you these things? And now you know what is holding him back, so that he may be revealed at the proper time. For the secret power of lawlessness is already at work; but the one who now holds it back will continue to do so till he is taken out of the way. And then the lawless one will be revealed, whom the LORD Jesus will overthrow with the breath of his mouth and destroy by the splendor of his coming. The coming of the lawless one will be in accordance with how Satan works. He will use all sorts of displays of power through signs and wonders that serve the lie, and all the ways that wickedness deceives those who are perishing. They perish because they refused to love the truth and so be saved. For this reason God sends them a powerful delusion so that they will believe the lie and so that all will be condemned who have not believed the truth but have delighted in wickedness.   2 Thessalonians 2:1-12

I will now explain what Jesus was making reference to, when he spoke to His disciples in John 14:1-3.

"Do not let your hearts be troubled. You believe in God; believe also in me. My Father's house has many rooms; if that were not so, would I have told you that I am going there to prepare a place for you? And if I go and prepare a place for you, I will come back and take you to be with me that you also may be where I am... I am the way and the truth and the life. No one comes to the Father except through me."

John 14:1-3

Jesus knew his Apostles would understand later on that He was making reference to the Jewish Galilean wedding and wants all disciples to be prepared, what-ever the year or hour. To illustrate this point, let us take a look at a preaching message within the next eleven to twelve pages by Jay McCarl, who has given me his ex-press permission to use in this book.

The Galilean Wedding. Jay McCarl 24.10.2020[1]

We must remember that two thirds of the gospel took place in a little strip of land next to the Sea of Galilee, so we cannot ignore the culture that was there.

Arranged wedding

Whilst the children were still young a father of the boy would spot what he thinks is another youngster, a girl, who would be a suitable future bride for his son.

Marriages were not to do with romance but to do with making a family stronger etc.

He arranges a feast and sends someone, possibly a close relative to the girl's father's house and knocks on the door saying that he has "Gospel", good news for him. Please would he come to a feast. The father would drop everything and would go there. The feast might last a day or two before he asks the girl's father if he is agreeable to his daughter getting engaged to his son. If he agrees then they immediately get in a scribe to write down two perfectly identical copies of what terms these two men have agreed on. This is called a "Ketubah". These copies might be written on pieces of pottery, skin or anything at hand.

Such items in the Ketubah would be:

1 The Galilean Wedding. Jay McCarl 24.10.2020. Link to the video: youtube.com/watch?v=JbO-BvyRVDU'

Price of the Bride – Ten donkeys, two sheep etc
Dowry – A gift to the Bride. Provided by the
Groom's father

This was something of value that would sustain the
Bride in the event of the Bridegroom dying or otherwise.

Children

How many children?
It could be that a childless Bride be considered
to have broken the terms of the Ketubah
It was considered shameful if a wife did not bear
children.

When these terms were agreed they would say
"Amen" and the scribe might sign his name at the bot-
tom and a copy given to the two fathers. The greater
copy to the Groom's father.

The two fathers would take their copies home and
place them in what we would call our family safe, but
they would call their family shrine (no idolatry) where
ceremonial plates etc were kept.

When the children were 14-15 the families would
communicate and decide to get the two publicly be-
trothed. On the appointed day the families would each
wake their child and dress them up in their nice clothes.
Family and friends would accompany them to the synagogue but each group separately at different times since

they were not allowed to see each other on the day of their betrothal.

They go to the synagogue to ceremoniously cleanse themselves. This was needed if there was going to be a very sacred occasion. This was done by going down seven steps into a hole in ground (Mikveh) which held rainwater. The water was about waist deep and considered "living water". The person would strip off and be naked. The individual would go down and crouch down in a fetal position so that their whole body was covered with the water. Then they would exit and dry off and get clothed again.

Since they were going into a sacred agreement with God, they wanted to be pure and holy. The Jews believed that man was born with a sinful nature, but whilst in the womb they had not yet sinned. Whilst in the womb they were immersed in water. They had an expression for this process, "Born Again!"

They return with their family to their house and then in their best clothes, family and friends they emerge with loud musical instruments and joy make their way to the village gate, which is where anything of importance happened. All the business was done there. This ceremony needed to have many witnesses.

A betrothal was a big event in the village and so many would come out to see this. A group of boys carrying poles and a cloth would come out. They would position the poles in a square with a brightly coloured cloth as a canopy – Called a "HUPPA". This is the canopy under which the betrothal ceremony would take place.

This canopy symbolised; When God met with the Children of Israel, he told them to cleanse themselves for three days. Moses went up the mountain and God came down. The Huppa symbolised God's glory coming down on the place of the covenant.

Under the Huppa stands the couple and the two fathers step forward. The betrothal begins. The betrothal legally weds the couple at this point. The actual wedding only takes place about a year later on.

The Ketubah is now brought out and read publicly. All the terms are listed so that everyone can hear them, and no one will be able to say that they didn't know that that detail was in there. The fathers agree that what was read was in their copy. The crowd then shouted "Amen" signifying their agreement and that they couldn't go back on this agreement.

Once this was read then the price of the Bride was read. (Remember the Apostle saying you were bought with a price?) The Groom's father brings in the price (donkeys etc) for the father of the Bride to inspect and ensure it was what was agreed. Once this is agreed by both fathers the crowd shouts "Amen".

Then the dowry is brought out. This is what the Bride's father brings out. This is in the form of coins.

The Bridegroom's father inspects it but doesn't keep it. It goes back to the other father. Once agreed the crowd shouts "Amen!"

The Bridegroom now gives the Bride gifts. These could be a ring, nose ring etc. If he was too poor to afford these, he would give her a bronze Putah, worth about 10p in todays currency. He has not just given her 10p, he has given her everything he has.

She would then give him a gift, we don't know what she might have given him.

Now a jug of wine is brought out by the Groom (pure wine) and he pours a cup of wine (this is known as "the cup of joy") and very reverently and respectfully he offers the cup to the Bride. This is an arranged marriage but at this juncture she has full authority to refuse the cup and push it away. If this happens then the wedding is off. There will probably be shouting and remonstrations from family and friends, but they will not be able to do anything about it since it is her right at this moment.

When and if the Bride takes the cup and has just a sip, she then passes it back to the Groom and he has a sip. The covenant has been ratified. The witnesses then shout "Amen". They are now officially married but they cannot live together at the moment.

They have now entered into a Covenant Relationship. According to Middle Eastern culture and Biblical thinking, they have become "One Flesh". This does not refer to a sexual union, it refers more to a DNA union where they are as much, brother and sister, even. The power of this relationship can be illustrated by two siblings being separated by distance and not being able to communicate for the rest of their lives. The relationship is only broken when one of them dies. This is the thought behind a Covenant Relationship. ….. Till death do us part!

Then the Bridegroom says, *"You are now covenanted to me by the laws of Moses and Israel, and I will not drink of this cup again until I drink it with you in the house of my father"*

At the last supper the disciples hear "Wedding" when he said these words.

The Bridegroom is handed a veil after this. He hands this to his Bride who puts it on. She will now wear this whenever she is outside. This signifies that she is promised to someone else. This also says that she is keeping herself pure for her Bridegroom.

The ceremony is over and all return home.

Now starts the Betrothal period.

They now start on projects that will take a year to complete.

The Galilean wedding was different to others in Israel. This was a surprise wedding. The Galileans were by nature rebels.

The Bride had to create a wedding dress. Lots of material was required and jewellery was needed. Lots of necklaces. She would have to barter with traders and source material for her dress which was massive.

The Bridegroom's father now has to make white linen robes for guests at the wedding. These are to honour the guests and also to show up any gate-crashers.

The son now had to build rooms onto his father's house (compound style).

He also has to acquire enough food to feed perhaps 100 guests for a few days of the feasting.

In my Father's house there are many rooms (Bridal chambers) and if it were not so I would have told you and I go there to prepare a place for you so that you may be there with me where I am.

The son prepares the rooms and gathers all the food for the feast. He knows that the wedding should take place about a year from the betrothal. The father inspects all the work and finally gives his approval. The final stage is now reached.

The Galilean wedding differed from others, only the Bridegroom's father knew the time of the ceremony.

No-one knows the day or the hour, not the angels in heaven, not even the Son of Man. Only the Father knows so you must be ready.

The Bridegroom doesn't know the day or the hour the wedding will take place so close the presumed time he sleeps with his wedding garments on in a room with the best man and groomsmen. The Bride is doing likewise. They are ready for the ceremony at a moment's notice.

The Bridegroom will ask his Father this *"Please let me get my Bride!"* obviously many times but his Father will only say *"When I think the time is right"*

The Son doesn't know the time neither does anyone else except the Father. What is known are the signs just before the wedding.

More than 500 of the 1000 plus prophecies in the bible have already been fulfilled literally and accurately. Because of that track record we can assume that the remainder will be fulfilled in the same way.

"Take heed that no one deceives you. For many will come in My name, saying, 'I am the Christ,' and will deceive many. And you will hear of wars and rumours of wars. See that you are not troubled; for all these things must come to pass, but the end is not yet" (Matthew 24:4-6). In other words, before the last days, we can expect long periods of deception and false teachers.

As we noted a moment ago, the first sign has four parts:

• Wars and nation rising against nation—World War I

was begun by two nations, then joined by the nations of the world.

- Famines because of the war, great plagues on the earth during and after World War I, followed by the Great Depression

- Pestilence—Millions died in Europe of the flu epidemic. US servicemen then brought this epidemic back with them after the war, and it reportedly took the lives of more than a million people in America. The COVID virus has already 104 million infections with 2.25M fatalities

- Earthquakes have increased in number all through the twentieth century and right up to today. The days are coming when they will become more devastating and cause greater destruction and more deaths than ever before. Our LORD did not teach that the end would come immediately. He said these earlier events would be "the beginning of sorrows"

A significant sign

The fact that the people of Israel have settled again in their ancestral homeland is a miracle in itself. No nation in world history has ever been able to maintain its national existence after having been removed from her national homeland for hundreds of years. No nation, that is, except Israel.

Another sign is:

Increase in Travel and Knowledge

The great falling away from God

Scoffers who ask "Where is the promise of His coming?"

Finally, one day within a day or two of the expected time, because food will go off, the Father will probably in the middle of the night, will go to his son and tell him to go and collect his bride.

Jesus said that He would return as a thief in the night. It was done in this way to show that it could take place at any time and the guests needed to be prepared.

The parable of the ten virgins and their lamps needing to be filled with oil underlines this principle.

The Son will then get a Shofar and blow it loudly outside. This will wake people in the village and the noise will get to the Bride's house. Only the wedding guests will be expecting this call and will be ready, dressed and will leave their house quickly to join the procession that is now taking place led by the Bridegroom on his way to collect his Bride. The groomsmen will dance around the groom singing songs and making a lot of noise pounding on doors waking up the neighbourhood.

The groomsmen will pick up a "Litter" and follow the Bridegroom shouting *"The Bridegroom is coming"*. *Blessed is he who comes in the name of the LORD"*.

The procession would serpentine through the village gathering the invited guests increasing the number.

They would then arrive at the Bride's house. She would be waiting outside with her bridesmaids holding oil lamps.

The groomsmen carrying the "Litter" place it in front of the Bride who then steps into it and they then lift her up off the ground and carry her. They now don't waste any time but take the shortest route to the Bridegroom's Father's house. This is known as *"Flying the Bride to the Father's house"*.

As soon as this procession gets to the Father's house and goes in, the doors are shut and locked. No-one can get out and no-one can get in. They have a feast for the next seven days. Note the seven years between rapture and second coming.

The Bridegroom takes a pouch with salt from his family's house and a pouch of salt from the Bride's and pours them out on a single plate and mixes them together (inseparable). He takes a piece of bread and dips it into the salt and gives one half of the bread to his Bride and the other piece he has. This is known as a Covenant of Salt. It ratifies the agreement.

He then takes the jug of wine, the pure wine, and the "Cup of Joy", takes the first sip and then hands it to his Bride. The party now shouts "Amen!".

He takes his Bride upstairs and they consummate the marriage. The party goes into high gear.

Revelation 19. I heard them shouting *"Hallelujah for the LORD God almighty reigns, let us be glad and rejoice and give Him glory for the marriage of the Lamb has come and the Bride has made herself ready".* John adds *"Fine linen white and clean was given her to wear".*

The question about the hope of the imminent return of Christ presented in John 14 and other theories, is which view best expresses the blessed hope of the Church and promotes and supports holy living, as we wait for the LORD. Read Titus 2:11-14.

I pray this gives you more hope and joy in the midst of the world crisis and helps you to realise it is important to get your heart right with God now. Do not think because you attend church or give to charity or are perceived by others as good, that is enough in itself to be chosen, because our LORD sees beyond that. Your faith has to be genuine because you will be tested.

The unwise are unprepared and sadly, as mentioned, that is about fifty per cent of those who attend churches today. To illustrate this point, I will use the Parable of the Wise and Foolish Virgins.

At that time the kingdom of heaven will be like ten virgins who took their lamps and went out to meet the bridegroom. Five of them were foolish and five were wise. The foolish ones took their lamps but did not take any oil with them. The wise ones, however, took oil in jars along with their lamps. The bridegroom was a long time in coming, and they all became drowsy and fell asleep. At midnight the cry rang out: 'Here's the bridegroom! Come out to meet him!' Then all the virgins woke up and trimmed their lamps. The foolish ones said to the wise, 'Give us some of your oil; our lamps are going out.' 'No,' they replied, 'there may not be enough for both us and you. Instead, go to those who sell oil and buy some for yourselves.' But while they were on their way to buy the oil, the bridegroom arrived. The virgins who were ready went in with him to the wedding banquet. And the door was shut. Later the others also came. 'LORD, LORD,' they said, 'open the door for us!' But he replied, 'Truly I tell you, I don't know you.' Therefore keep watch, because you do not know the day or the hour.

Matthew 25:1-13

Just like in the days of Noah, when God regretted creating 'man', there were so many warning signs to prove God was not pleased with the people of Sodom and Gomorrah. God loves all people but hates our sins. People were having weddings and other celebrations as normal, then in a short space of time, God's wrath of destruction overcame them, no-one unrighteous survived. Their corrupt type of lifestyle was never God's intention for mankind, whom He made in His own image. The people of Sodom and Gomorrah had gone too far to the extent that they were consumed in so much wrong doings and depravity, that they themselves could no longer see it, hence, no confession or repentance. Arrogance to do whatever evil they wanted, including orgies with the same gender and gang rape was not an issue for them. The whole city was defiled and became an abomination to God.

> *Do not have sexual relations with a man as one does with a woman; that is detestable.*
>
> Leviticus 18:22

> *The acts of the flesh are obvious: sexual immorality, impurity and debauchery; idolatry and witchcraft; hatred, discord, jealousy, fits of rage, selfish ambition, dissensions, factions and envy; drunkenness, orgies, and the like. I warn you, as I did before, that those who live like this will not inherit the kingdom of God.*
>
> Galatians 5:19-21

> *…But the cowardly, the unbelieving, the vile, the murderers, the sexually immoral, those who practice magic arts, the idolaters and all liars — they will be consigned to the fiery lake of burning sulfur. This is the second death.*
>
> Revelation 21:8

Sodom and Gomorrah did not want what was considered just, rather evil in the eyes of the LORD. When your hearts become so hardened to sin's deceitfulness, you become arrogant with your sin to the point of lawlessness and parading it publicly, each doing what they please, like the people of Israel who made the golden calf in rebellion to the living God. Rebellion is witchcraft and these men had clearly forgotten the God who had delivered them from bondage, through Moses when God saved them from slavery in Egypt. When you witness carnality in this form, it is enough to make a righteous person physically sick. A righteous person would not only want to separate themselves from such a place and people, but would never want to look back.

It appears Lot's wife, did not understand why they had gone from a great city to a very small town. She dishonored God by pushing His mercy back into His face when she looked back and desired in her heart, such a wicked city whose people were full of witchcraft.

> But about that day or hour no one knows, not even the angels in heaven, nor the Son, but only the Father. As it was in the days of Noah, so it will be at the coming of the Son of Man. For in the days before the flood, people were eating and drinking, marrying and giving in marriage, up to the day Noah entered the ark; and they knew nothing about what would happen until the flood came and took them all away. That is how it will be at the coming of the Son of Man. Two men will be in the field; one will be taken and the other left. Two women will be grinding with a hand mill; one will be taken and the other left.
>
> Matthew 24:36-41

The question is, did Lot know his wife loved the riches of Sodom despite its great sin? Was Lot's wife against Lot in his views? Jesus said, *"no-one who puts his hand to the plow and looks back is fit for the Kingdom"*, Luke 9:62. It is easy to judge Lot's wife but reflect for a minute and ask yourself, 'am I sometimes wishing I could experience the past enjoyments which is sinful in the eyes of God and the righteous?' If your right eye causes you to stumble, pluck it out. Similarly, if your right hand causes you to sin, cut it off, Matthew 5:29-30.

> *Brothers and sisters, I do not consider myself yet to have taken hold of it. But one thing I do: Forgetting what is behind and straining toward what is ahead, I press on toward the goal to win the prize for which God has called me heavenward in Christ Jesus.*
>
> Philippians 3:13-14

How about Lot's two sons-in-law, pledged to marry his daughters, and who did not take his warning to get out of Sodom seriously? In those days, a son-in-law, where possible, would have worked in their father's business. Were they set to profit from Lot's wealth? Were they laughing at Lot like in the days of Noah, where many would have mocked Noah when he was building the ark to save him and his family? How is it they allowed their future wives to leave without them? There may have been division in Lot's household which would have brought about further loneliness for Lot and his daughters, nevertheless, you can see the real issue was not about whether they agreed or disagreed with their friend's immorality, but who was saved or unsaved. What good was it for Lot's sons-in-law to gain the whole world yet lose their very soul? Mark 8:36. In which direction are you looking today?

> Brothers and sisters, we do not want you to be uninformed about those who sleep in death, so that you do not grieve like the rest of mankind, who have no hope. For we believe that Jesus died and rose again, and so we believe that God will bring with Jesus those who have fallen asleep in him. According to the LORD's word, we tell you that we who are still alive, who are left until the coming of the LORD, will certainly not precede those who have fallen asleep. For the LORD himself will come down from heaven, with a loud command, with the voice of the archangel and with the trumpet call of God, and the dead in Christ will rise first. After that, we who are still alive and are left will be caught up together with them in the clouds to meet the LORD in the air. And so we will be with the LORD forever. Therefore encourage one another with these words.
>
> 1 Thessalonians 4:13-18

How to be free from loving the world?

1. Put God first, spend as much time every day in God's word and meditation on His wonders. If you have young children, read the Bible with them during your daily devotions

2. Take twenty to forty minutes each day to play instrumental Christian soaking music and lay down to help you sense God's presence

3. Avoid deception and sin. Where possible, stay away from temptation and ask the Holy Spirit to help keep you from falling into it. Follow Joseph's example in Genesis chapters 37-50 and Job's in Job 31:1. See also James 1:27

4. In particular, spend less time on your smart phone and social media platforms, which could lure your senses back into the world

5. Be accountable to a Christian brother or sister who is awake and ready

6. Pray with small Christian groups who are alert and prepared

7. Watch and listen to weekly prophecy updates by J.D Farag (www.jdfarag.com) and Jimmy Evans (endtimes.substack.com). I also encourage you to study the book of Revelation and to aid your studies, I signpost you to a book by Dr. Arnold G Fruchtenbaum, titled The Footsteps of the Messiah: Revised 2020 Edition

8. Serve the LORD wholeheartedly, hold the things of this world lightly, live each day as though it is the last, and live a repentant and holy life

Prayer

Dear God, thank You for encouraging me through Your holy Scriptures. I repent of looking back. Please help me tear down any idols in my life and be more grateful for my salvation. I pray for those who are left behind at the rapture, that they will turn away from evil and unbelief and look up to You. Help me to be like the five wise virgins and always be ready to be caught up and joined to Christ forever! In Jesus' name. Amen.

CHAPTER 7

❧ LONELY SOLDIERS IN THE END TIMES ❧

One day the older daughter said to the younger, "Our father is old, and there is no man around here to give us children—as is the custom all over the earth. Let's get our father to drink wine and then sleep with him and preserve our family line through our father."

Genesis 19:31-32

The question to ask here is, where are we in God's prophetic calendar? Are we the last generation? Is Pope John Francis the last Pope? Will there be loneliness of true Christianity following the formation under the Pope of a one world church? Only God knows for sure. However, the way things are going, it appears that the scene is being set for the anti-christ to make his appearance sooner than we may care to think. When twisted and perverse things are called the 'norm', then Sodom is here.

But mark this: There will be terrible times in the last days. People will be lovers of themselves, lovers of money, boastful, proud, abusive, disobedient to their parents, ungrateful, unholy, without love,

*unforgiving, slanderous, without self-control, brutal,
not lovers of the good, treacherous, rash, conceited,
lovers of pleasure rather than lovers of God—having
a form of godliness but denying its power. Have
nothing to do with such people.*

2 Timothy 3:1-5

As I write, red heifers are in the process of being proved unblemished, ready to be sacrificed in the forthcoming third temple, which is about to be built in Israel. Although most Christians and Messianic Jewish people will know, it is Jesus who became our sacrificial lamb and paid the price for our sins once and for all, whereas, most unbelieving Israel are still awaiting their Messiah. In the meantime, they feel the need to build a new temple, so they can atone for their sins. It is then, the anti-christ will appear during the Tribulation and claim to be God, causing most to flee when they realise he is not, because of the wicked things he will start to do. Read Ezra 3:1-6, Matthew 24:15-21, 2 Thessalonians 2:1-4 and Revelation 13:5-6. False prophets are already appearing in Israel and only time will tell when these prophesies will come to past. False teachers give false hope. Even Jesus, who committed no sin, mentioned we should discern the signs.

Every soldier in battle at some stage feels lonely and needs encouragement. Are you feeling alone in a crowd? You could be praying about the world situation and feel battle-weary. And like Lot, may be unsure which direc-

116

tion to take. You may even be ashamed to tell anyone what you believe is going to happen to this world, for fear of being ridiculed. It is important not to lean on your own understanding but trust the LORD with all your heart, Proverbs 3:5-6.

I will use Lot and his daughters at this point of the story, to represent those people who may be left behind after the rapture and are in a state of perplexity at the sudden loss of loved-ones and seeing the world being destroyed in the Tribulation. Imagine what it is like to lose your loved ones and all your possessions suddenly. Remember the story of Job, how he lost everything except his wife overnight. As a consequence of Lot's original lustful choices and the death of Lot's wife, Lot would have felt lonelier as a widower than ever before. He was now old, financially poor with two adult single daughters to care for. This was not what he planned. Lot's daughters also became lonely. Sadly, all three of them were all led to flee and live in a cave, isolated from the world. During the middle of the seven-year Tribulation, when the Jewish community suddenly realise the anti-christ is not the true Messiah, they will also run away to hide in caves.

As Jesus was sitting on the Mount of Olives, the disciples came to him privately. "Tell us," they said, "when will this happen, and what will be the sign of your coming and of the end of the age?" Jesus answered: "Watch out that no one deceives you. For many will come in my name, claiming, 'I am the

Messiah,' and will deceive many. You will hear of
wars and rumors of wars, but see to it that you are
not alarmed. Such things must happen, but the end
is still to come. Nation will rise against nation, and
kingdom against kingdom. There will be famines
and earthquakes in various places. All these are the
beginning of birth pains.

Then you will be handed over to be persecuted and
put to death, and you will be hated by all nations
because of me. At that time many will turn away
from the faith and will betray and hate each other,
and many false prophets will appear and deceive
many people. Because of the increase of wickedness,
the love of most will grow cold, but the one who
stands firm to the end will be saved. And this gospel
of the kingdom will be preached in the whole world
as a testimony to all nations, and then the end will
come.

 So when you see standing in the holy place 'the
abomination that causes desolation, 'spoken
of through the prophet Daniel—let the reader
understand— then let those who are in Judea flee to
the mountains. Let no one on the housetop go down
to take anything out of the house. Let no one in the
field go back to get their cloak. How dreadful it will
be in those days for pregnant women and nursing
mothers! Pray that your flight will not take place in
winter or on the Sabbath. For then there will be great

distress, unequaled from the beginning of the world
until now — and never to be equaled again.

Matthew 24:3-21

After the Church is taken up to celebrate the wedding feast for seven years in heaven, the Time of Jacob's Trouble will begin (2 Thessalonians 2:1-12). There will again be two types of people; those whose eyes are opened and choose eternal life through Jesus Christ and some who will refuse to repent and choose to follow the beast. Read Revelation 6:15-17; 9:20; 16:11 and 19:17-18. Those who run away from the anti-christ and decline his mark, will undoubtedly be persecuted, some even killed. But they will never need to dread losing their salvation and will immediately be taken to heaven and given white robes. Revelation 6:9-11; 7:9-10; 14:4 and 17:14. The final battle which is called Armageddon (Revelation 19:11-21), takes place on the plains of Megiddo in Israel. It states that hundreds of thousands of soldiers will be massed on this plain to conquer Jerusalem and destroy Israel. Jesus on His return with His Bride (the saints – Zechariah 14), will wage war against the anti-christ, false prophet and his followers at the Armageddon. Jesus Christ will win and He will reign with His saints for a millennium, Revelation 20. Although Satan will be loosed from captivity for a short time, him, the anti-christ, false prophet and all their followers will, in the end be cast with him in the lake of fire forever, where there will be grating of teeth.

Who would think that freedom from Sodom would have led to more sin with three members of a family? I

119

cannot imagine it ever crossed Lot's mind to have sexual intercourse with his daughters, the children he brought up from birth in Sodom and Gomorrah. However, there is a saying, you can take the people out of the gutter but you cannot take the gutter out of the people. Lot's daughters only knew the ways of Sodom and Gomorrah, to do what you want to get your way and have your pleasure instead of trusting God for His provision. Instead of Lot's daughters praying to God for new husbands, which the God of miracles could have provided for them, they forced their own father to get drunk so they could sleep with him in order to continue the family line. This type of sin is known as incest, Leviticus 18:7-18, which is not only wrong in the eyes of God but illegal in the eyes of most of the world.

The question is, were Lot's daughters hearts veiled? Lot's eyes were covered again, that is for sure, as deception crept in. Full national lockdown can be likened to being in a cave, unable to see anyone else from a different household. If it went on for years and years, imagine the two-daughter scenario, conspiring to get their dad drunk in their desperate attempt to have children. How absolutely absurd and a great sin against God. This could happen during the seven-year Tribulation. The anti-christ, who will head the new world order, could demand everyone to lock down and only obey his ungodly commands. Then during this time, people could be forced to take the mark of the beast through a pill or injection. The forthcoming 'one world' health organisation could oversee every nation, forcing their subjects to take a drug, which alters your DNA and which the world at that point may believe it is a cure for the terrible diseases and plagues which are about to come upon the world during the Tribulation, Revelation 6:8. The Nephilim (both angel and man), otherwise known as giants in the Bible, were not pure human-beings. God had to become human, through the person of Christ, so He could save human-kind. If the human-race's DNA is altered, they cannot be redeemed. Therefore, if you receive the mark of the beast, you cannot be saved.

> A third angel followed them and said in a loud voice:
> "If anyone worships the beast and its image and
> receives its mark on their forehead or on their hand,
> they, too, will drink the wine of God's fury, which
> has been poured full strength into the cup of his
> wrath. They will be tormented with burning sulfur
> in the presence of the holy angels and of the Lamb.
> And the smoke of their torment will rise for ever and
> ever. There will be no rest day or night for those who
> worship the beast and its image, or for anyone who
> receives the mark of its name."
>
> Revelation 14:9

Author and Minister, Reverend Andrew Baguley mentioned in his book, The Tyranny of Evil, that God's DNA is all over our unique DNA. When uncoded, it spells the ancient name of God, YHWH, meaning, "I AM WHO I AM" (Exodus 3). Sadly, many will die by the very drug they thought would heal them. The word pharma means sorcery. See Revelation 18:23. The nations will be deceived by the one world pharmaceutical establishment. Like Lot was intoxicated by alcohol, so his daughters could control the narrative, those who are left behind and love their life more than God, will feel they have lost control.

The tragedy of Lot's daughters' shameful act was that their sons formed the Moabite and Ammonite nations (Deuteronomy 23:3-6), who became enemies of Israel's descendants and who God wanted to later destroy until there was no-one left, Zephaniah 2:8-9.

Lot may have pondered over his past choices and consequently died a lonely old man. However, at least he finally understood that living in the fear of God in humble surroundings is far better than living wealthy without God in calamity and anarchy, which is like not living at all, Proverbs 28:6. I have every confidence Lot, like his uncle Abraham, will be in paradise. Apart from reading Luke 16:19-31, I know Paradise exists, as I was shown by the LORD through a personal body transported-like vision. Paradise is perfect, unlike this fallen earth. I can only describe it to be like what the Garden of Eden once was when Adam and Eve first walked with God. That is, perfect temperature, beautiful, serene, tranquil, safe and secure under God's watch and protection. Then after The Judgement Day, we will cross over to live in God, who will be our light forever. Read Isaiah 60:19-22 and Revelation 22:5.

The Lonely Soldier poem which is in the Appendix was written a long time ago, which I had forgotten I kept to one side with my scrap writings of this book several years after and as a result, it was omitted from my book of poems called 'The Cry of a Londoner'. I realise now that this was not by coincidence but rather a God-incidence.

So where are we heading? We can all learn a great deal from Lot's story. We can all quarrel with our relatives, loved-ones and neighbours over things in hindsight seem trivial in comparison to our actual relationship with them. Sometimes you need to check your motives for arguing and be humble enough to back down or come to an amical agreement which honours both parties because no-one is better than the other. Whatever you choose, seek God's counsel first rather than let lust be the deciding factor.

Abraham was considered righteous and called a friend of God (James 2:23), because of his sincere faith in God. Lot, however, eventually learned the hard way, that it was better to be like Abraham.

Whilst in worship with Prayer Storm live online in April 2020, I heard these words:

"Fish in a bowl; fish in a bucket".

Then Ezekiel 36:23-36 came to mind and my interpretation back then was: "Although God was referring to Israel at that time, I sense like when we take fish out of murky, unclean waters in order to wash the fish bowl and place the fish temporarily in a bucket of water before placing the fish back in a clean bowl of water, this is what the LORD is doing to the nations. I sense He is cleansing our hearts and whilst doing so, some of us are frightened of the unknown, resisting change and knocking into one another, not comprehending that the will of God through these temporary changes is to mould us. Although I am not saying God started this current pandemic, I believe He is allowing it for a reason and for a season. If you read the book of Ezekiel, in line with other prophets, God's main purpose for scattering His people is to remind us that we are dependent on Him and not some of the idols we've created in our lives. It's always first and foremost to point us to the living God who shares His glory with no other. Who and what are you depending on today? Look up! The LORD is doing something new in us - cleansing and softening hearts around the world - ready for the big harvest."

For I know that God works for the good of those who love Him and to whom He has called for His purpose.
Romans 8:28

I also believe the LORD is shaking the nations; He is changing the Church as we know it. Did Jesus intend the Body of Christ to become like an entertainment industry, whereby the congregation sit in pews or chairs in even rows, facing the front, watching a pastor or preacher on the stage, speaking on a microphone every Sunday? Not that this is wrong per se, but are you the true worshippers God is seeking, worshipping in truth and in spirit? (John 4:24). The book of Acts is the best illustration of how Jesus wants His Church to look like until He returns. Anything else could get us into legalism and we run the risk of no longer being led by the Spirit of God but by flesh, including the pressures of being state-run.

> For the LORD called some to be Apostles, Prophets, Evangelists, Pastors and Teachers ...(my emphasis)
> Ephesians 4:11.

I believe the LORD is resetting the true Church in these last days, so we see the Five-fold ministry emerging like never before to strengthen what remains. The Social Media platforms have allowed those who hold these offices, like Jarren Lewis and AoC Network, to be seen and heard. Whereas in the past, only the pastor or vicar was taken seriously as having the main role in the Body of Christ, along with a few members of supporting staff. I believe the underground church, similar to that in China, is emerging and small churches will meet in homes and undercover outlets with no official name, where the presence of God can truly manifest to prepare the children of God to be a mighty army for Christ in these End Times.

Ask yourself today and be truthful, 'is the nation in which I reside full of righteous people?' And 'are there more than ten people who are righteous, and if so, am I one of them?' The issue is not whether three or four were found righteous in Sodom but sadly not only did Abraham's intercession stop at ten people, there were not even five righteous people to be found. Are you among the righteous in your city? If so, then make the most of the time to intercede for your nation like Abraham, because the days we are living in are becoming more evil than Sodom and Gomorrah.

Are we in an invisible war zone? Is the world being reset? If so, who is resetting it? Will everything we do be online? Will the world become a Communist state before Jesus Christ returns to rule and reign? These are questions no-one can correctly answer except God. National resetting is not a new thing, only the Israelites were obeying God for the purpose of holiness and not wickedness. We can learn in Leviticus 25 about the Year of Jubilee. Even if certain men feel they can rule the world without God, I know only God holds the future in His hands.

> Count off seven sabbath years—seven times seven
> years—so that the seven sabbath years amount to
> a period of forty-nine years. Then have the trumpet
> sounded everywhere on the tenth day of the seventh
> month; on the Day of Atonement sound the trumpet
> throughout your land. Consecrate the fiftieth year
> and proclaim liberty throughout the land to all its
> inhabitants. It shall be a jubilee for you; each of you
> is to return to your family property and to your own
> clan. The fiftieth year shall be a jubilee for you; do not
> sow and do not reap what grows of itself or harvest

*the untended vines. For it is a jubilee and is to be
holy for you; eat only what is taken directly from the
fields.*

*In this Year of Jubilee everyone is to return to their
own property.*   Leviticus 25:8-13

We will also see more false prophets arising in these
last days when men and women state their word is specifically from God when in fact it is not and they know it.
Jesus warned us about such people.

*...and many false prophets will appear and deceive
many people.*   Matthew 24:11

In fact we are witnessing much of Jesus' prophecies
including massive earthquakes in Turkey and bordering
Syria (known as Damascus in the Bible, Isaiah 17:1).

*There will be great earthquakes, famines and
pestilences in various places, and fearful events and
great signs from heaven.*   Luke 21:11

This scripture came to my mind as Tim and I were
having our devotional during lockdown.

*'Take a bunch of hyssop, dip it into the blood in the
basin and put some of the blood on the top and on
both sides of the doorframe. None of you shall go
out of the door of your house until morning. When
the LORD goes through the land to strike down the
Egyptians, he will see the blood on the top and sides*

> *of the doorframe and will pass over that doorway, and*
> *he will not permit the destroyer to enter your houses*
> *and strike you down.'* Exodus 12:22–23

I am not suggesting the literal act but could the LORD have been trying to tell us something in the run up to Passover 2020? I felt I should share this for you to weigh up. Then to confirm this word, two years afterwards, I read the extract below in Jimmy Evan's Tipping Point article:

What do you do when you're preparing to leave? How should we act as we wait for the further fulfilment of Bible prophecy or even the Rapture? The Old Testament book of Exodus has one suggestion for us.

It has to do with yeast, or in biblical terms, leaven.

Back then, the Israelites had been enslaved in Egypt. God was preparing to rescue his people. Led by Moses, they were going to escape Egypt.

Based on God's instructions, Moses gave a series of specific directions to the Israelites about the very first Passover. Among other things, he told them to get rid of all the leaven in their houses, before they celebrated that sacred meal.

> *Seven days you shall eat unleavened bread. On the*
> *first day you shall remove leaven from your houses.*
> *For whoever eats leavened bread from the first day*
> *until the seventh day, that person shall be cut off*

from Israel. On the first day there shall be a holy convocation, and on the seventh day there shall be a holy convocation for you. No manner of work shall be done on them; but that which everyone must eat—that only may be prepared by you. So you shall observe the Feast of Unleavened Bread, for on this same day I will have brought your armies out of the land of Egypt. Therefore you shall observe this day throughout your generations as an everlasting ordinance. Exodus 12:15-17

Moses told the people to get rid of the old leaven in their homes—every bit of it—in preparation for Passover, and in preparation for their journey. The people were about to set out for new lives in the Promised Land, and they needed to clean out their cupboards before they left...

In addition to the word in Exodus, I had a dream in 2020, which involved the need of a chip implant in our hand in order to make transactions in the workplace. I also sensed in the dream that it was a time when we were facing a virus more serious than the recent pandemic. We happened to be reading Jeremiah, 2 Kings, 2 Chronicles - no coincidence, it talks about King Josiah tearing down all the idols.

About ten months after my above dream, I was shown a news article in the Mail Online. This is the heading:

Would you have a microchip implanted under your SKIN? 3,000 Swedes with electronic tags embedded into their hands risk their personal data being 'used against them'

- More than 3,000 Swedish people have a tiny microchip embedded in their hand

- The implants let them pay for shopping, enter buildings and book train tickets

- Several companies in Sweden offer the service to their employees for free

- A scientist has warned that those using the service are at risk of data breaches

---

Since this article, I am sure you have read more recent news about the microchip in various other places around the world. In USA, something similar is used on mental health patients in hospital. Is the vaccine or pill a method the anti-christ will use to get to the people during the Tribulation? Or will he use a combined digital ID mechanism, forced by an emergency stimulus, like food, energy, financial, or climate crisis, which without this ID, no-one can either buy or sell? There is talk that the new electric cars may be fitted with chips and how do we know mobile phones do not already contain them, so people can be controlled. Is this preparing the world for the new social credit scoring and ultimately the Mark of the Beast, which is 666? J. D Farag mentioned in his prophecy update, that the technology is advancing so fast, that it will surpass the one described in the Book of Revelation within ten years. I think, we can all agree with this and it shows we do not have long before Jesus returns? With Artificial Intelligence (AI) on the increase and some elite thinking they can live forever their way and not God's way, just like during the Tower of Babel, they are in for a severe shock.

I sense we need to concentrate on the goodness of God and embrace His victory, rather than the mark of the beast. When we focus on Jesus, the author and finisher of our faith, we will have confidence to obtain the seal of God's name on our foreheads, Revelation 22:4.

Are we also moving nearer to the time where Israel will have to get ready to defend herself? If we look at the Bible prophecies, all have been fulfilled except the rapture and all that follows in terms of the tribulation and the anti-christ. If we take a look at what the world should be like prior to the rapture, it is exactly like it is today.

Ezekiel 38 will soon be fulfilled. At the moment, Russia, Iran and Turkey who want to see the total destruction of Israel, have enough soldiers and fire power to fulfil this prophecy. However, Egypt, Jordan and Syria are not mentioned in this prophecy, so they must have made a peace deal with Israel. A similar peace agreement, called The Abraham Accords, is what has happened in August 2020 with the help of the USA creating a peace agreement with these nations (United Arab Emirates).

We are definitely in the last days, even in the toe nails of the large statue in King Nebuchadnezzar's dream interpreted by Prophet Daniel. Thankfully, God is never fearful. He wants you to look to Him, whose Kingdom will have no end. No-one knows their time and hour, so live every day as though it is the last (Proverbs 27:1). Make sure you die or live in Christ.

I cannot help but imagine how great the feast in heaven will be and how you would never be alone or feel lonely ever again. The big heavenly feast will be full of God's joyful children, celebrating with music, food, dance and singing, with Jesus at the centre, bringing peace, security and warming you with His undying love.

God will never leave you nor forsake you. Your unique fingerprint is proof that you are God's handiwork. If you are experiencing multiple suffering, do not think God has finished with you, rather He has just started a good work in you, which He will complete. God sings over you. Jesus is your hope of salvation – your real solution out of this mess.

Whatever is going on, Jesus went through worse and can sympathise with your pain and anguish. In Revelation 5:5, one of the elders said to the Apostle John, "Do not weep! See, the Lion of the tribe of Judah, the Root of David, has triumphed...". God is in control even in a messy world. It is important to know whatever your lot, The LORD will safely bring you Home! Be still and know He is God! Jesus will never leave you alone. Jesus is your Rock, He is constant; never let your gaze come away from His forever!

Practical things you may want to do in order to prepare for the Last Days reset

1. Surround yourselves with born-again followers of Christ you can trust to uphold you in prayers. Share the Holy Communion together, sing praise and worship songs and speak to each other with Psalms and scriptures that comfort and build each other up and keep your eyes fixed on Jesus our LORD and Saviour. Meditate on Psalm 139, knowing God's presence is always with you

2. Meditate on the Holy Bible and pray more in the Spirit daily in order to build up your spirit-man

3. Prepare for persecution, which is bound to take place prior to the rapture. Always remember to pray for the salvation of the original root, Israel (Romans 11)

4. Prepare for the consequences of wars, natural disasters and government control measures, which could lead to food and energy shortages. Even Joseph prepared for the seven-year famine (Genesis 41 & 47). Therefore, it is prudent to keep about three months' supply in cool storage, extra non-perishable food in cupboards for rainy days or grow your own organic fruit and vegetables. Keep spare blankets and warm clothing

5. Invest money in a Christian independent bank which is not subject to the state. Also, consider investing in small amounts of gold or silver

6. Purchase or keep onto a small number of valuable items, which you can barter with

7. Submit to authority but do not compromise your faith by submitting to the enemy's lies

8. Do not accept the mark of the beast (Revelation 13). Read up on your Common Law rights. Teach your children about persecution and to stand firm in their faith

9. Be joyful always, pray continually putting on the full armor of God (Ephesians 6:10-18); and give thanks in all circumstances, for this is God's will for you in Christ Jesus (1 Thessalonians 5:16-18). Remember, you are set apart for such a time as this

10. Encourage yourself in the LORD like King David, and keep on sharing your faith in all situations (1 Peter 3:15), in the hope that any loved-ones left behind, will not take the mark of the beast (Revelation 13:15-18)

11. For those left behind after the rapture, place a copy of Jimmy Evans' book, 'Where are the Missing People?' on a table or conspicuous area where loved-ones will find it

12. Remember, you are not alone, The LORD will never leave you nor forsake you. Keep watch, for The Day of Salvation is near!

 Prayer

Dear God, thank you for encouraging me through Your holy Scriptures. Help me not to panic but rather look up. Your perfect love casts out fear (1

John 4:18). Please help me to encourage my fellow brothers and sisters in Christ. Help me to forgive whoever may betray and hurt me. I pray for those who are left behind, especially my loved ones. May your remnant turn to You in the Last Days. I am looking forward to being with the saints, seeing Your Face, being in Your glorious light and part of the One-New-Man, the New Jerusalem forever! In Jesus' name. Amen.

❧ APPENDIX I ❧

I wrote the poem, 'The Lonely Soldier' in 2012 and unknowingly filed it in a different place to where I would normally have kept my poetry. Hence, why it did not get published in The Cry of a Londoner, book of poems in 2017. I now realise, the LORD allowed me to omit this particular poem because He had use for it in this book during this time and season. This is how I chose the title of this book. The Hebrew words for my poem title is 'Chayal Boded'.

The Lonely Soldier Poem

> *I stand in the dark, misty cold*
> *Wondering who will be with me when I grow old,*
> *Not a dicky bird to be seen*
> *It's still, quiet and no tambourine,*
> *I'm all alone with my rifle by my side,*
> *In the dark and muddy fields, with nowhere to hide,*
> *No friend, no family, no whisper to be found*
> *All have abandoned me or is it the other way round?*
> *My feet feel weary, in shoes which aren't mine*
> *My knees buckle with fear as I'm in the frontline,*
> *I never really know from one day to the next*

Whether my life will be taken or can I still send a
text,

"Texting who?" I ask, that's the big question
I pretend as to fit in, so not to appear lonesome,
It's playing games with my mind, this living in
denial

Not wanting to face up to life's big trial,
Who will be there for me, when the war is over?
Who will be in the car to pick me up from Dover?
Who will cuddle me and play catch up stories?
Who will hold my hand and laugh at the past oldies?
Who will dress my wounds when my back needs a
fix?

Who will cook me a hot meal and pour me a cup of
Horlicks?

Who will listen to the horror stories I've to tell?
Who will give me medicine when I'm unwell?
Who will correct me when I go wrong?
Who will mourn for me when I am gone?
I guess I have to trust in the only One I know
The One who carried me with His footprints in the
snow,

Yes, Daddy God will always be there for me
He's the only One who always helps me see,
Things aren't always what they seem

No matter how ugly the theme,
He always helps you get wiser and bolder
So, I can stand up and say, I'm not the lonely soldier.

By Tope Pearson, 24th November 2012

❧ APPENDIX II ❧

Additional End Time Scriptures

*The word of the LORD came to me: "Son of man,
set your face against Gog, of the land of Magog, the
chief prince of Meshek and Tubal; prophesy against
him and say: 'This is what the Sovereign LORD
says: I am against you, Gog, chief prince of Meshek
and Tubal. I will turn you around, put hooks in your
jaws and bring you out with your whole army—your
horses, your horsemen fully armed, and a great horde
with large and small shields, all of them brandishing
their swords. Persia, Cush and Put will be with
them, all with shields and helmets, also Gomer with
all its troops, and Beth Togarmah from the far north
with all its troops—the many nations with you.*

*"'Get ready; be prepared, you and all the hordes
gathered about you, and take command of them.
After many days you will be called to arms. In future
years you will invade a land that has recovered from
war, whose people were gathered from many nations
to the mountains of Israel, which had long been
desolate. They had been brought out from the nations,*

and now all of them live in safety. You and all your troops and the many nations with you will go up, advancing like a storm; you will be like a cloud covering the land.

"'This is what the Sovereign LORD says: On that day thoughts will come into your mind and you will devise an evil scheme. You will say, "I will invade a land of unwalled villages; I will attack a peaceful and unsuspecting people—all of them living without walls and without gates and bars. I will plunder and loot and turn my hand against the resettled ruins and the people gathered from the nations, rich in livestock and goods, living at the center of the land." Sheba and Dedan and the merchants of Tarshish and all her villages will say to you, "Have you come to plunder? Have you gathered your hordes to loot, to carry off silver and gold, to take away livestock and goods and to seize much plunder?"'

"Therefore, son of man, prophesy and say to Gog: 'This is what the Sovereign LORD says: In that day, when my people Israel are living in safety, will you not take notice of it? You will come from your place in the far north, you and many nations with you, all of them riding on horses, a great horde, a mighty army. You will advance against my people Israel like a cloud that covers the land. In days to come, Gog, I will bring you against my land, so that the nations may know me when I am proved holy through you before their eyes.

*"'This is what the Sovereign LORD says: You are
the one I spoke of in former days by my servants the
prophets of Israel. At that time they prophesied for
years that I would bring you against them. This is
what will happen in that day: When Gog attacks
the land of Israel, my hot anger will be aroused,
declares the Sovereign LORD. In my zeal and fiery
wrath I declare that at that time there shall be a
great earthquake in the land of Israel. The fish in
the sea, the birds in the sky, the beasts of the field,
every creature that moves along the ground, and
all the people on the face of the earth will tremble
at my presence. The mountains will be overturned,
the cliffs will crumble and every wall will fall to the
ground. I will summon a sword against Gog on all
my mountains, declares the Sovereign LORD. Every
man's sword will be against his brother. I will execute
judgment on him with plague and bloodshed; I will
pour down torrents of rain, hailstones and burning
sulfur on him and on his troops and on the many
nations with him. And so I will show my greatness
and my holiness, and I will make myself known in
the sight of many nations. Then they will know that I
am the LORD.'*   Ezekiel 38

*Do not call conspiracy
everything this people calls a conspiracy;
do not fear what they fear,
    and do not dread it.
The LORD Almighty is the one you are to regard as
holy,*

he is the one you are to fear,
   he is the one you are to dread.
He will be a holy place;
   for both Israel and Judah he will be
a stone that causes people to stumble
   and a rock that makes them fall.
And for the people of Jerusalem he will be
   a trap and a snare.   Isaiah 8:12-14

A shoot will come up from the stump of Jesse;
   from his roots a Branch will bear fruit.
The Spirit of the LORD will rest on him—
   the Spirit of wisdom and of understanding,
   the Spirit of counsel and of might,
   the Spirit of the knowledge and fear of the
LORD—
and he will delight in the fear of the LORD.
He will not judge by what he sees with his eyes,
   or decide by what he hears with his ears;
but with righteousness he will judge the needy,
   with justice he will give decisions for the poor of
the earth.
He will strike the earth with the rod of his mouth;
   with the breath of his lips he will slay the wicked.
Righteousness will be his belt
   and faithfulness the sash around his waist.
The wolf will live with the lamb,
   the leopard will lie down with the goat,
the calf and the lion and the yearling together;
   and a little child will lead them.

The cow will feed with the bear,
  their young will lie down together,
  and the lion will eat straw like the ox.
The infant will play near the cobra's den,
  and the young child will put its hand into the
viper's nest.
They will neither harm nor destroy
  on all my holy mountain,
for the earth will be filled with the knowledge of the
LORD
  as the waters cover the sea.
In that day the Root of Jesse will stand as a banner
for the peoples; the nations will rally to him, and his
resting place will be glorious. In that day the LORD
will reach out his hand a second time to reclaim the
surviving remnant of his people from Assyria, from
Lower Egypt, from Upper Egypt, from Cush, from
Elam, from Babylonia, from Hamath and from the
islands of the Mediterranean.
He will raise a banner for the nations
  and gather the exiles of Israel;
he will assemble the scattered people of Judah
  from the four quarters of the earth.
Ephraim's jealousy will vanish,
  and Judah's enemies will be destroyed;
Ephraim will not be jealous of Judah,
  nor Judah hostile toward Ephraim.
They will swoop down on the slopes of Philistia to the
west;
  together they will plunder the people to the east.

They will subdue Edom and Moab,
  and the Ammonites will be subject to them.
The LORD will dry up
  the gulf of the Egyptian sea;
with a scorching wind he will sweep his hand
  over the Euphrates River.
He will break it up into seven streams
  so that anyone can cross over in sandals.
There will be a highway for the remnant of his people
  that is left from Assyria,
as there was for Israel
  when they came up from Egypt. Isaiah 11

A prophecy against Damascus:
"See, Damascus will no longer be a city
  but will become a heap of ruins." Isaiah 17:1

In those days and at that time,
  when I restore the fortunes of Judah and Jerusalem,
I will gather all nations
  and bring them down to the Valley of Jehoshaphat.
There I will put them on trial
  for what they did to my inheritance, my people
Israel,
because they scattered my people among the nations
  and divided up my land.
They cast lots for my people
  and traded boys for prostitutes;
  they sold girls for wine to drink.

Now what have you against me, Tyre and Sidon and
all you regions of Philistia? Are you repaying me for
something I have done? If you are paying me back, I
will swiftly and speedily return on your own heads
what you have done. For you took my silver and
my gold and carried off my finest treasures to your
temples. You sold the people of Judah and Jerusalem
to the Greeks, that you might send them far from
their homeland.

"See, I am going to rouse them out of the places to
which you sold them, and I will return on your own
heads what you have done. I will sell your sons and
daughters to the people of Judah, and they will sell
them to the Sabeans, a nation far away." The LORD
has spoken.

Proclaim this among the nations:
    Prepare for war!
Rouse the warriors!
    Let all the fighting men draw near and attack.
Beat your plowshares into swords
    and your pruning hooks into spears.
Let the weakling say,
    "I am strong!"
Come quickly, all you nations from every side,
    and assemble there.

Bring down your warriors, LORD!
"Let the nations be roused;

let them advance into the Valley of Jehoshaphat,
for there I will sit
to judge all the nations on every side.
Swing the sickle,
for the harvest is ripe.
Come, trample the grapes,
for the winepress is full
and the vats overflow —
so great is their wickedness!"

Multitudes, multitudes
in the valley of decision!
For the day of the LORD is near
in the valley of decision.
The sun and moon will be darkened,
and the stars no longer shine.
The LORD will roar from Zion
and thunder from Jerusalem;
the earth and the heavens will tremble.
But the LORD will be a refuge for his people,
a stronghold for the people of Israel.

Blessings for God's People
"Then you will know that I, the LORD your God,
dwell in Zion, my holy hill.
Jerusalem will be holy;
never again will foreigners invade her.

"In that day the mountains will drip new wine,
and the hills will flow with milk;

all the ravines of Judah will run with water.
A fountain will flow out of the LORD's house
   and will water the valley of acacias.
But Egypt will be desolate,
   Edom a desert waste,
because of violence done to the people of Judah,
   in whose land they shed innocent blood.
Judah will be inhabited forever
   and Jerusalem through all generations.
Shall I leave their innocent blood unavenged?
   No, I will not."
The LORD dwells in Zion!   Joel 3:1-21

But I will encamp at my temple
   to guard it against marauding forces.
Never again will an oppressor overrun my people,
   for now I am keeping watch.

The LORD their God will save his people on that day
   as a shepherd saves his flock.
They will sparkle in his land
   like jewels in a crown.   Zach 9:8 & 16

A day of the LORD is coming, Jerusalem, when your
possessions will be plundered and divided up within
your very walls.

I will gather all the nations to Jerusalem to fight
against it; the city will be captured, the houses

ransacked, and the women raped. Half of the city will go into exile, but the rest of the people will not be taken from the city. Then the LORD will go out and fight against those nations, as he fights on a day of battle. On that day his feet will stand on the Mount of Olives, east of Jerusalem, and the Mount of Olives will be split in two from east to west, forming a great valley, with half of the mountain moving north and half moving south. You will flee by my mountain valley, for it will extend to Azel. You will flee as you fled from the earthquake in the days of Uzziah king of Judah. Then the LORD my God will come, and all the holy ones with him.

On that day there will be neither sunlight nor cold, frosty darkness. It will be a unique day—a day known only to the LORD—with no distinction between day and night. When evening comes, there will be light.

On that day living water will flow out from Jerusalem, half of it east to the Dead Sea and half of it west to the Mediterranean Sea, in summer and in winter.
The LORD will be king over the whole earth. On that day there will be one LORD, and his name the only name.

The whole land, from Geba to Rimmon, south of Jerusalem, will become like the Arabah. But

Jerusalem will be raised up high from the Benjamin Gate to the site of the First Gate, to the Corner Gate, and from the Tower of Hananel to the royal winepresses, and will remain in its place. It will be inhabited; never again will it be destroyed. Jerusalem will be secure.

This is the plague with which the LORD will strike all the nations that fought against Jerusalem: Their flesh will rot while they are still standing on their feet, their eyes will rot in their sockets, and their tongues will rot in their mouths. On that day people will be stricken by the LORD with great panic. They will seize each other by the hand and attack one another. Judah too will fight at Jerusalem. The wealth of all the surrounding nations will be collected — great quantities of gold and silver and clothing. A similar plague will strike the horses and mules, the camels and donkeys, and all the animals in those camps.

Then the survivors from all the nations that have attacked Jerusalem will go up year after year to worship the King, the LORD Almighty, and to celebrate the Festival of Tabernacles. If any of the peoples of the earth do not go up to Jerusalem to worship the King, the LORD Almighty, they will have no rain. If the Egyptian people do not go up and take part, they will have no rain. The LORD will bring on them the plague he inflicts on the

*nations that do not go up to celebrate the Festival of
Tabernacles. This will be the punishment of Egypt
and the punishment of all the nations that do not go
up to celebrate the Festival of Tabernacles.
On that day holy to the LORD will be inscribed on
the bells of the horses, and the cooking pots in the
LORD's house will be like the sacred bowls in front
of the altar. Every pot in Jerusalem and Judah will
be holy to the LORD Almighty, and all who come to
sacrifice will take some of the pots and cook in them.
And on that day there will no longer be a Canaanite
in the house of the LORD Almighty.*

Zechariah 14

*Then Daniel went to Arioch, whom the king had
appointed to execute the wise men of Babylon,
and said to him, "Do not execute the wise men of
Babylon. Take me to the king, and I will interpret his
dream for him."*

*Arioch took Daniel to the king at once and said, "I
have found a man among the exiles from Judah who
can tell the king what his dream means."*

*The king asked Daniel (also called Belteshazzar),
"Are you able to tell me what I saw in my dream and
interpret it?"*

*Daniel replied, "No wise man, enchanter, magician
or diviner can explain to the king the mystery he has
asked about, but there is a God in heaven who reveals*

mysteries. He has shown King Nebuchadnezzar what will happen in days to come. Your dream and the visions that passed through your mind as you were lying in bed are these:

"As Your Majesty was lying there, your mind turned to things to come, and the revealer of mysteries showed you what is going to happen. As for me, this mystery has been revealed to me, not because I have greater wisdom than anyone else alive, but so that Your Majesty may know the interpretation and that you may understand what went through your mind. "Your Majesty looked, and there before you stood a large statue—an enormous, dazzling statue, awesome in appearance. The head of the statue was made of pure gold, its chest and arms of silver, its belly and thighs of bronze, its legs of iron, its feet partly of iron and partly of baked clay. While you were watching, a rock was cut out, but not by human hands. It struck the statue on its feet of iron and clay and smashed them. Then the iron, the clay, the bronze, the silver and the gold were all broken to pieces and became like chaff on a threshing floor in the summer. The wind swept them away without leaving a trace. But the rock that struck the statue became a huge mountain and filled the whole earth.

"This was the dream, and now we will interpret it to the king. Your Majesty, you are the king of kings. The God of heaven has given you dominion and

power and might and glory; in your hands he has placed all mankind and the beasts of the field and the birds in the sky. Wherever they live, he has made you ruler over them all. You are that head of gold.

"After you, another kingdom will arise, inferior to yours. Next, a third kingdom, one of bronze, will rule over the whole earth. Finally, there will be a fourth kingdom, strong as iron—for iron breaks and smashes everything—and as iron breaks things to pieces, so it will crush and break all the others. Just as you saw that the feet and toes were partly of baked clay and partly of iron, so this will be a divided kingdom; yet it will have some of the strength of iron in it, even as you saw iron mixed with clay. As the toes were partly iron and partly clay, so this kingdom will be partly strong and partly brittle. And just as you saw the iron mixed with baked clay, so the people will be a mixture and will not remain united, any more than iron mixes with clay.

"In the time of those kings, the God of heaven will set up a kingdom that will never be destroyed, nor will it be left to another people. It will crush all those kingdoms and bring them to an end, but it will itself endure forever. This is the meaning of the vision of the rock cut out of a mountain, but not by human hands—a rock that broke the iron, the bronze, the clay, the silver and the gold to pieces.

154

"The great God has shown the king what will take place in the future. The dream is true and its interpretation is trustworthy."   Daniel 2:24-45

When you see 'the abomination that causes desolation' standing where it does not belong—let the reader understand—then let those who are in Judea flee to the mountains. Let no one on the housetop go down or enter the house to take anything out. Let no one in the field go back to get their cloak. How dreadful it will be in those days for pregnant women and nursing mothers! Pray that this will not take place in winter, because those will be days of distress unequaled from the beginning, when God created the world, until now—and never to be equaled again. If the LORD had not cut short those days, no one would survive. But for the sake of the elect, whom he has chosen, he has shortened them. At that time if anyone says to you, 'Look, here is the Messiah!' or, 'Look, there he is!' do not believe it. For false messiahs and false prophets will appear and perform signs and wonders to deceive, if possible, even the elect. So be on your guard; I have told you everything ahead of time.

But in those days, following that distress,
the sun will be darkened,
   and the moon will not give its light;
the stars will fall from the sky,
   and the heavenly bodies will be shaken.'

*At that time people will see the Son of Man coming
in clouds with great power and glory. And he will
send his angels and gather his elect from the four
winds, from the ends of the earth to the ends of the
heavens.*

*Now learn this lesson from the fig tree: As soon as its
twigs get tender and its leaves come out, you know
that summer is near. Even so, when you see these
things happening, you know that it is near, right
at the door. Truly I tell you, this generation will
certainly not pass away until all these things have
happened. Heaven and earth will pass away, but my
words will never pass away.*

The Day and Hour Unknown

*But about that day or hour no one knows, not even
the angels in heaven, nor the Son, but only the
Father. Be on guard! Be alert! You do not know when
that time will come. It's like a man going away: He
leaves his house and puts his servants in charge,
each with their assigned task, and tells the one at the
door to keep watch. "Therefore keep watch because
you do not know when the owner of the house will
come back—whether in the evening, or at midnight,
or when the rooster crows, or at dawn. If he comes
suddenly, do not let him find you sleeping. What I
say to you, I say to everyone: 'Watch!'*

Mark 13:14-37

Once, on being asked by the Pharisees when the kingdom of God would come, Jesus replied, "The coming of the kingdom of God is not something that can be observed, nor will people say, 'Here it is,' or 'There it is,' because the kingdom of God is in your midst."

Then he said to his disciples, "The time is coming when you will long to see one of the days of the Son of Man, but you will not see it. People will tell you, 'There he is!' or 'Here he is!' Do not go running off after them. For the Son of Man in his day will be like the lightning, which flashes and lights up the sky from one end to the other. But first he must suffer many things and be rejected by this generation.
"Just as it was in the days of Noah, so also will it be in the days of the Son of Man. People were eating, drinking, marrying and being given in marriage up to the day Noah entered the ark. Then the flood came and destroyed them all.

It was the same in the days of Lot. People were eating and drinking, buying and selling, planting and building. But the day Lot left Sodom, fire and sulfur rained down from heaven and destroyed them all.

It will be just like this on the day the Son of Man is revealed. On that day no one who is on the housetop, with possessions inside, should go down to get them. Likewise, no one in the field should go back for anything. Remember Lot's wife! Whoever tries to keep their life will lose it, and whoever loses their life will preserve it. I tell you, on that night two people will be in one bed; one will be taken and the other left. Two women will be grinding grain together; one will be taken and the other left."

"Where, LORD?" they asked. He replied, "Where there is a dead body, there the vultures will gather."
Luke 17:20-37

When these things begin to take place, stand up and lift up your heads, because your redemption is drawing near. Luke 21:28

...live soberly, righteously, and godly in the present age, looking for the blessed hope and glorious appearing of our great God and Savior Jesus Christ.
Titus 2:12-13

Dear friends, this is now my second letter to you. I have written both of them as reminders to stimulate you to wholesome thinking. I want you to recall the words spoken in the past by the holy prophets and the command given by our LORD and Savior through your apostles.

Above all, you must understand that in the last days

scoffers will come, scoffing and following their own evil desires. They will say, "Where is this 'coming' he promised? Ever since our ancestors died, everything goes on as it has since the beginning of creation." But they deliberately forget that long ago by God's word the heavens came into being and the earth was formed out of water and by water. By these waters also the world of that time was deluged and destroyed. By the same word the present heavens and earth are reserved for fire, being kept for the day of judgment and destruction of the ungodly.

But do not forget this one thing, dear friends: With the LORD a day is like a thousand years, and a thousand years are like a day. The LORD is not slow in keeping his promise, as some understand slowness. Instead he is patient with you, not wanting anyone to perish, but everyone to come to repentance.

But the day of the LORD will come like a thief. The heavens will disappear with a roar; the elements will be destroyed by fire, and the earth and everything done in it will be laid bare.

Since everything will be destroyed in this way, what kind of people ought you to be? You ought to live holy and godly lives as you look forward to the day of God and speed its coming. That day will bring about the destruction of the heavens by fire, and the elements will melt in the heat. But in keeping with his promise we are looking forward to a new heaven and a new earth, where righteousness dwells.

*So then, dear friends, since you are looking forward
to this, make every effort to be found spotless,
blameless and at peace with him. Bear in mind that
our LORD's patience means salvation, just as our
dear brother Paul also wrote you with the wisdom
that God gave him. He writes the same way in all his
letters, speaking in them of these matters. His letters
contain some things that are hard to understand,
which ignorant and unstable people distort, as they
do the other Scriptures, to their own destruction.
Therefore, dear friends, since you have been
forewarned, be on your guard so that you may not
be carried away by the error of the lawless and fall
from your secure position. But grow in the grace and
knowledge of our LORD and Savior Jesus Christ. To
him be glory both now and forever! Amen.*

2 Peter 3

*Dear friends, although I was very eager to write to
you about the salvation we share, I felt compelled
to write and urge you to contend for the faith that
was once for all entrusted to God's holy people. For
certain individuals whose condemnation was written
about long ago have secretly slipped in among you.
They are ungodly people, who pervert the grace of
our God into a license for immorality and deny Jesus
Christ our only Sovereign and Lord.
Though you already know all this, I want to remind
you that the Lord at one time delivered his people
out of Egypt, but later destroyed those who did*

not believe. And the angels who did not keep their positions of authority but abandoned their proper dwelling—these he has kept in darkness, bound with everlasting chains for judgment on the great Day. In a similar way, Sodom and Gomorrah and the surrounding towns gave themselves up to sexual immorality and perversion. They serve as an example of those who suffer the punishment of eternal fire. In the very same way, on the strength of their dreams these ungodly people pollute their own bodies, reject authority and heap abuse on celestial beings. But even the archangel Michael, when he was disputing with the devil about the body of Moses, did not himself dare to condemn him for slander but said, "The Lord rebuke you!" Yet these people slander whatever they do not understand, and the very things they do understand by instinct—as irrational animals do—will destroy them.

Woe to them! They have taken the way of Cain; they have rushed for profit into Balaam's error; they have been destroyed in Korah's rebellion.

These people are blemishes at your love feasts, eating with you without the slightest qualm—shepherds who feed only themselves. They are clouds without rain, blown along by the wind; autumn trees, without fruit and uprooted—twice dead. They are wild waves of the sea, foaming up their shame; wandering stars, for whom blackest darkness has been reserved forever.

Enoch, the seventh from Adam, prophesied about them: "See, the Lord is coming with thousands upon thousands of his holy ones to judge everyone, and to convict all of them of all the ungodly acts they have committed in their ungodliness, and of all the defiant words ungodly sinners have spoken against him. "These people are grumblers and faultfinders; they follow their own evil desires; they boast about themselves and flatter others for their own advantage.

A Call to Persevere

But, dear friends, remember what the apostles of our Lord Jesus Christ foretold. They said to you, "In the last times there will be scoffers who will follow their own ungodly desires." These are the people who divide you, who follow mere natural instincts and do not have the Spirit.

But you, dear friends, by building yourselves up in your most holy faith and praying in the Holy Spirit, keep yourselves in God's love as you wait for the mercy of our Lord Jesus Christ to bring you to eternal life.

Be merciful to those who doubt; save others by snatching them from the fire; to others show mercy, mixed with fear—hating even the clothing stained by corrupted flesh.

To him who is able to keep you from stumbling and to present you before his glorious presence without fault and with great joy— to the only God our Savior be glory, majesty, power and authority, through Jesus Christ our Lord, before all ages, now and forevermore! Amen.   Jude 3-25

I am coming soon. Hold on to what you have, so that no one will take your crown.   Revelation 3:11

❧ Appendix III ❧

Prayer of Salvation (or Recommitment Prayer)

Father God, I realise that I have sinned in thought word and deed and as a result, there is a barrier between you and me, that only your Son Jesus can break. Please forgive me of my past sins and wash me clean, so that I can start a relationship with you, through Jesus and enter into a new life on this earth, knowing I have a place in Heaven.

I can't do this on my own, but I ask you LORD Jesus to help, guide, forgive and restore me, so that I can have eternal life with you. I believe that Jesus died and rose again to set me free. I realise that it is by grace I have been saved and not by any good works I have done, but I thank you Jesus that you will guide me, be my friend, Saviour and LORD of all my life. I ask you to download your Holy Spirit in me today, so I can start this journey with you, hear your voice and understand your will for my life. In Jesus name. Amen.

❧ BIBLIOGRAPHY ❧

Because the Time is Near, John MacArthur, 2007

God's Glorious Promise, Andrew Baguley and Roger French, 2013

The Rock, the Road and the Rabbi, Kathie Lee Gifford with Rabbi Jason Sobel, 2018

The Tyranny of Evil, Andrew Baguley, 2021

The Doctrine of the Rapture, Dr Arthur F Green, 2021

After Covid, what? – Now what's being pulled out of the hat?, Andrew Baguley, 2022

The Galilean Wedding, Jay McCarl, 2020 (Sermon Transcript)

❧ MEET THE AUTHOR ❧

Tope Pearson, commissioned Itinerant Preacher, qualified as an Accountant by profession, and is Founder of the 'You Fit Perfectly' ministry, The Precious Foundation, a UK charity which cares for orphans around the world, Co-Founder of Equipping the Saints Ministries, a Speaker and Author of numerous books: Debt Revelation – Do Not Look Back; You Fit Perfectly; Why are you Running?; The Cry of a Londoner; The Wedding Dress; Heal to Health; and The Lonely Soldier. All these books can be purchased at www.youfitperfectly.co.uk or via leading online bookstores including Amazon and Barnes & Noble.

Tope receives invitations to speak and minister at various different churches during their Sunday service or breakfast/lunch meetings. If you would like to book her for speaking engagements, please send an email for consideration to: bookings@youfitperfectly.co.uk

Please follow on **Facebook**:

📘 @Youfitperfectly

📘 @EquippingtheSaintsMinistriesUK

For Equipping the Saints, please go to:

🌐 www.etsministries.org.uk

Please follow on **Instagram**:

📷 @you.fit.perfectly

Please subscribe to **YouTube** channel:

▶️ @youfitperfectly7436

▶️ @etsministries3166

If you would like to donate to orphans around the world, please visit: www.preciousfoundation.org.uk

❧ BOOKS BY TOPE ❧

Great Britain is sitting on over a one trillion pounds' debt – a time bomb just waiting to explode! What does God, our Creator say about all this? Is Britain living in a 'virtual reality'? This book was written by Tope Pearson in 2005 as a wake-up call for all who have been blinded to the spiritual implications of debt being so rife in our society, especially in the Church and reveals how it damages our health and divides families. It seeks to point out the relevant scriptures required for better and deeper spiritual understanding of debt. By meditating on God's Word, which should always be the last Word, and following the suggested practical solutions, it will help everyone who no longer wants to remain in debt, to find a way out. God is a God of second chances and wants to give everyone a fresh start in life. Read this book of debt revelation and do not look back!

Is it possible for a person to suffer through the loss of a parent; abuse, rejection, denial, debt, divorce, despair and disaster from being one of the victims in the 7/7 London Transport bombing, where 52 people lost their lives, and end up positive? First published in 2010, Tope Pearson who has been instrumental in changing thousands of lives for the good, tells the story of her journey from once upon a time not knowing who she was and feeling like a misfit in society, to knowing exactly who she is in her Creator. Read the book, be encouraged with her unique story and find out where you fit yesterday, today and forever.

He is one of the most famous and successful so-called wimps in both adult and children history, who likes running although not very good at it. He is the only man on earth who does not eat fish, except they eat him, yet a hero for coming out alive and changing the course of history for 120,000 souls and more. In this illuminating use of Yonah's (Jonah's) journey, Tope Pearson unfolds the reality about why so many of us find ourselves running away from our purpose in life. This book published in 2015, allows the reader, both Jew and Gentile, to see we all have choices in life and that life can be likened to running a race, but there are different routes for every unique individual. Whatever direction we choose to run, we should expect consequences that come from choosing it. As a result of Yonah's life changing episode, Tope reveals how we also can be liberated from the risk of spiritual deprivation and get back on track. The book also explores current day warnings and signs of the End Time and highlights the importance of true repentance and trust in God. Challenging and thought provoking for the times we are living in, 'Why are you Running?' will change the way you view home, death, commitment, your past, judgement and your call to ministry.

London is the centre of the UK's political and financial system. The year 2017 (Jewish calendar 5777) has been a significant year and we are living in turbulent times. The God of Abraham, Isaac and Jacob is calling out to us, if only we would listen. How long can we embrace deaf ears? Most of Tope Pearson's poems serve to illustrate a reminder that although we live in a fallen world, our greatest yearning is eternal love. The only true place to find such undying love is through the One who gives us the hope of salvation, that is, our LORD Jesus Christ – He is LOVE.

There are many men and women who long for a life partner chosen by God. There are some who get blessed, some who compromise and some who wait.

This is a story of trials and tribulations but also waiting faithfully. Using the events around the falling of the Jericho Wall as a backdrop, Tope Pearson gives her own account of taking God at His word and stepping out in faith, even though the writer's actions seemed crazy in the eyes of the world. This is a book every woman and man should read especially when they are searching for a marriage partner or need inspiration in the area of their faith.

There could never be a better time for concise information on general wellbeing as we live in a paradox world. In this booklet, published 2021, Tope Pearson seeks to introduce overall health issues from a Godly perspective, looking at body, soul and spirit. Tope uses her personal experience to give practical tips and includes bible scriptures and prayers which the reader may find useful. Why not learn or otherwise be reminded of how to stay well or obtain healing in your time of need.

Discipleship Manuals

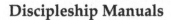

There are many Christians who have remained converts in our churches today and have not developed their full potential in Christ. This manual written by Tope in conjunction with her husband Tim, and published 2022, prepares the reader to develop a one-to-one discipleship relationship, by looking at the different elements of the Bible, the challenges and changes in our personal walk, in order to enable our brothers and sisters to understand the power of Jesus Christ in us. John 8:32-33. This booklet is to be used in conjunction with the Discipleship Manual, which should be purchased separately for the disciple.

Do you feel lonely in your church environment?

Many churches are not awake to the end times we are currently living in. The Lonely Soldier offers encouragement and solutions.

There is a lot of deception in the world today, with the mainstream media hiding the truth, along with world leaders preparing the way for the antichrist. As disciples of Jesus Christ, we need to be prepared and watchful, keeping our lamps burning, Luke 12 v 35.

This book by Tope Pearson, published 2023, provides practical tips on how to be able to stand firm in your Christian-Messianic faith during these End Times.

The Lonely Soldier, **along with** *The Cry of a Londoner; The Wedding Dress;* **and** *Heal to Health* **are all available to purchase as E-Books online.**